Translating Words,
Translating Cultures

Translating Words, Translating Cultures

Lorna Hardwick

Duckworth

This impression 2004
First published in 2000 by
Gerald Duckworth & Co. Ltd.
90-93 Cowcross Street
London EC1M 6BF
Tel: 020 7490 7300
Fax: 020 7490 0080
inquiries@duckworth-publishers.co.uk
www.ducknet.co.uk

Permission to quote from the works of modern writers is gratefully
acknowledged. Complete details of the published sources are
given in the text, notes and bibliography ad loc.

A catalogue record for this book is available
from the British Library

ISBN 0 7156 2912 3

Printed and bound in Great Britain by
Antony Rowe Ltd, Eastbourne

Contents

Acknowledgements

The research on which most of this book is based has been presented and discussed at various conferences, and I have particularly benefited from the comments and suggestions of participants at the Meetings of the International Society of the Classical Tradition in Boston, 1995 and Tübingen, 1998; the Triennial Meeting of the Hellenic and Roman Societies, Cambridge, 1997; the January Research Conferences at the Open University, Milton Keynes; the Classical Association, 1999; the Warburg Institute Seminar on the Classical Tradition, 1999. Part of Chapter 2 is based on my chapter 'Women, Translation and Empowerment' in *Women, Scholarship and Criticism* (Manchester University Press 2000), and parts of Chapters 5 and 6 are based on my articles prepared for the *International Journal of the Classical Tradition*. I thank the editors for their co-operation. I also thank the Arts Faculty of the Open University for research support grants and the Library staff at the Open University and at the Joint Library of the Hellenic and Roman Societies at the Institute of Classical Studies in London for their assistance.

I have gained tremendously from debate with my research students, past and present, and from colleagues and friends in several countries, many of whom sent me information or discussed their work in progress with me. Special thanks to Marcia Blumberg, P.J. Conradie, John Gregson, Edith Hall, Ruth Hazel, Fiona Macintosh, Kenneth MacKinnon, Marianne McDonald, Kai Merten, Margaret Mezzabotta, Des O'Rawe, Jan Parker, Stephen Regan, Peter Robinson, Chris Stray, Oliver Taplin, Simeon Underwood, Dennis Walder, Jennifer Wallace, Steve Woodward, to the series editors Susanna Morton Braund and Paul Cartledge, and to Deborah Blake of Duckworth.

Finally, I owe a great debt to Carol Gillespie, IT co-ordinator for the

Acknowledgements

Reception of Classical Texts Research Project at the Open University, for her unfailing patience and efficiency.

May 2000   Lorna Hardwick

1

The Battles of Translation

The batalis and the man I wil discrive
Fra Troys boundis first that fugitive
By fait to Ytail come and cost Lavyne

In 1513 Gavin Douglas (?1475-1522) completed his translation of
Vergil's *Aeneid*, although it was not published until 1553 (posthumously).
If you are not familiar with written Scots, try reading it aloud and then
compare the sound and rhythm with a mid-twentieth-century version
of the same lines, first published in 1952:

> I tell about war and the hero who first from Troy's frontier,
> Displaced by destiny, came to the Lavinian shores,
> To Italy
>
> C. Day Lewis, *The Aeneid of Virgil*

Finally, if you read aloud an even more recent version of the opening
lines of Vergil's epic you will have a third, very different, experience:

> I sing of arms and of the man, fated to be an exile, who long since
> left the land of Troy and came to Italy to the shores of Lavinium.
>
> David West, *Virgil: The Aeneid*

In these three versions, all the translators are recognisably dealing
with the same words; all might be said to be accurate translations; yet
all are both obviously and more subtly different from each other in
tone, rhythm and effect. This suggests that lexical 'accuracy' and
'faithfulness' to the original are not sufficient as descriptions of a fine
and influential translation (which all three may lay claim to be). The
aim of this book is to explore some of the ways in which writers and
translators have responded to poetry which was originally written in

9

Latin or Greek. To do this it is necessary to do more than just look at the original text (the source text) and see how the words are conveyed in the language of the translator (the target language). The relationship between the ancient (source) language and the target language is shaped by the translator in terms of his or her purpose in writing. It is also shaped by the way in which the target reader or audience is perceived and by the writer's judgement about how the impact of the Greek or Latin lines can effectively be communicated to those living in and through another language and another culture. There is also, of course, the role of the translator's interpretation of the wider meaning of the source text, both in its own time and for later readers. This aspect raises big questions about how the translator/writer views the relationship between ancient and modern, not just in terms of language but also in terms of values and ideas. The relationship between the two texts is also shaped by the readers or audience, who receive the new version and in their turn give it meaning.

Douglas' translation of Vergil is important in a number of ways, not least because of the immediate impact of its plain direct language on the reader/listener. Douglas was a pioneer. He wrote before the Renaissance had made translation of Latin writers a fashionable activity. He was therefore, less constrained by 'models' than were, for example, those translating Vergil after Dryden (1697) or Homer after Pope (*Iliad* 1715-20, *Odyssey* 1725-6). Perhaps because he knew that his work would be seen as a first attempt to translate a classical epic into Scots (or indeed English, although Chaucer had produced shorter passages), Douglas addressed the problems of the translator in his Prologue to Book 1. In his discussion, he combined pride in the capacity of the Scots language to communicate Vergil's poetry ('… this buke I dedicait / Writtin in the language of Scottis natioun', *Prologue* I, 102-3) with a slightly apologetic attitude to its roughness compared to the Latin. So in one respect Douglas is a very early example of the vernacular revival of the early Renaissance. Translating classical texts became a sign of linguistic vigour and independence, with the receiving language gaining additional dignity and authority by demonstrating its role in the transmission of classical learning.

Douglas did not discuss precisely the type of audiences and readers he had in mind. However, his Prologue discussions show that he did aim at a wide audience, not just princes and the powerful (for whom his other works were written) but also illiterate people who could respond to the poem when it was read aloud and children who were studying Vergil at school. These aims were helped by the plain rather than ornate words and phrases he used. He also included in his poem some explanatory phrases, sometimes almost amounting to a commentary on the significance of Vergil's characterisation and images. I use the words 'his poem' advisedly, because of course as well as producing a translation of Vergil, Douglas created a new work, a poem in its own right. His prologues emphasised the process of creativity, which is very evident in passages such as those dealing with the relationship between Dido and Aeneas, where Dido is given a more direct role with speeches which express her ardour and suffering through rhythm as well as words. In so doing, Douglas used the Scots language in telling ways, as well as communicating what he identified as the themes underlying the main emphases in Vergil. Commentators have pointed out how, as well as giving the Scots language status by association with Vergil, he also made Scots more flexible and brought about exchange of words and phrases with English (Tudeau-Clayton, 1999 against Canitz, 1996). Ironically, the main effect of Douglas' work on the literary development of Scots was delayed until the eighteenth-century literary revival.[1]

Douglas, who was briefly Bishop of Dunkeld, left his country for London, was accused of treason by the Scottish Lords of Council and died in exile. Yet in the scope and ambition of his poem he was not only in advance of the Elizabethan translators of classical poetry; he also addressed many of the problems concerning the relationship between ancient and 'modern' cultures with which current writers are battling. In this century Ezra Pound said of Douglas that 'he gets more out of Virgil than any other translator', a double-edged comment which points to the role of creativity if a translation is to achieve poetic status in its own right.

A look at some of the main features of translations of classical works in the second half of the twentieth century shows that, while this has been a time of exceptional variety and versatility in response to Greek and Latin writers, critical response has to some extent been polarised between those concerned primarily with the source text and those concerned with response to the new work. Sometimes this debate degenerates into conflict between the 'scholarly' and the 'poetic' and loses sight of the main function of a translation from classical poetry,

11

which is to provide a contemporary means of understanding and responding to the ancient work. In so doing, the translation redirects attention to the source text, and tests it. Edwin Morgan has addressed this aspect in the preface to his play *Phaedra*, which is based on Racine's *Phèdre*: 'In this translation I have used a Glaswegian based Scots ... partly hoping that the non-classical shock of it will bring the characters back alive, and aiming also ... to find out what there is in this most remarkable play that survives and transcends a jolt into an alien register' (Morgan, 2000, p. 8). Morgan's translation also gives status to Scots as a language of the emerging Scottish classical theatre, in contrast to Liz Lochhead's *Medea* (2000) which restricts Scots to a dialect spoken by the servile figures of the Nurse and the Tutor.

The second half of the twentieth century has seen three main trends in published translations of classical works. The first was the emergence of a sequence of modern translations into English of the epic poetry of Homer and Vergil, of Horace and the other major Latin poets and of Greek drama, both tragedy and comedy. It might almost be said that this represents canonical translations of canonical texts. This activity has been counterbalanced by a second and more recent trend: an increase in interest in lesser known authors, periods and themes such as love poetry and pastoral.[2] The third trend is the creative blurring of the distinction between different kinds of translations, versions, adaptations and more distant relatives. This is especially evident in the often dynamic use of classical images, texts and myths by poets and dramatists such as Tony Harrison, Seamus Heaney, Ted Hughes, Liz Lochhead, Christopher Logue, Michael Longley, Derek Walcott and Timberlake Wertenbaker.

The framework within which these developments have taken place is one in which comparatively few general readers can comfortably read Latin in the original, while fewer still are at home with Greek. The focus on translations of canonical texts grew from recognition that Homer, Vergil and Greek tragedy are important both for general readers and for students and academics in subject disciplines other than classics – literature and drama, for instance. So there are further questions underlying debates about the quality of different translations: what kind of reader is a particular translation created for? For example, the series of parallel texts and translations developed by the Loeb Classical Library catered for those with a limited knowledge of the language and for historians and philosophers wanting to refer to literal translations of ancient evidence, that is translations which followed the source text closely and as far as possible translated words in the same order. The best of these translations also communicate something of the literary quality of the original, but it was not part of the intention of the series to create works of independent literary status or even, necessarily, to provide a 'good read'.

Producing a translation which was readable and which attempted to remove what were perceived as unnecessary barriers between reader and ancient text was a prime aim of the Penguin Classics series. E.V. Rieu's translation of the *Odyssey* (1946) sold over 100,000 copies in the first few months and in fifty years sold over three million. His *Iliad* (1950) sold one and a half million. The publisher's early publicity material made the point that unnecessary difficulties were created by 'erudition, the archaic flavour and foreign idiom that render so many existing translations repellent to modern taste' (discussed by Underwood, 1998, p. 50). This signalled both the desire to reach a popular market and the rejection of the view that differences between ancient cultures, values and modern versions could be communicated by using language which at times seemed archaic and thus emphasised what was 'alien' or 'different' about Greek or Roman culture. Rieu's language was therefore simple, plain and unadorned, avoiding lengthy sentences or hyperbole. Sometimes the effect is bathetic, as in his version of the striking image of the horses of Patroclus who mourn his death, refusing to move – 'the son of Cronos when he saw their grief was sorry for them' (*Iliad* XVII, Rieu p. 328) or 'When Achilles heard this he sank into the black depths of despair' (*Iliad* XVIII, Rieu p. 337). Direct speech was made colloquial (with the ironic result of dating it). Most important of all, the translation was in prose, not verse. Some critics, predictably, felt that what they traditionally saw as 'the freshness and nobility' of Homer was lost. Nobility was one of the four qualities of Homer which the nineteenth-century poet and critic Matthew Arnold thought that translators of Homer should convey; the others were rapidity, plainness and directness (in syntax, words and thought).[3]

More recently the main feature of Homer's style has been reformulated as 'immediacy'. This concept includes use of concrete rather than abstract language, the effect being to relate the heroic to everyday life. To achieve this, Homeric epic used stylistic features such as stock scenes (in battle for instance), formulaic epithets repeated to describe a particular figure ('swift-footed Achilles') and extended similes which linked images of the everyday worlds of the audience to the imagined world of the poem.[4] This analysis of course has implications for rhythm and verse form as well as word choice and metaphor and focuses attention on the nature of the Homeric text itself.

These are issues considered by Walter Shewring in the Epilogue on Translation which accompanies his prose translation of the *Odyssey* (1980, pp. 299-330). Shewring's discussion covers difficulties of idiom in both Greek and English, verse forms and rhythms, rhymes, metre (and especially its effect on choice of words). He also addresses the cultural influence of translations as well as specific points about Homeric style and the conventions of oral poetry (from which the Homeric poem as we have it developed). Shewring is particularly enlightening when discussing the difficulties of communicating the range of meanings associated with particular Greek words, such as *agathos* (good, but also well-born, brave, skilled) especially when the one English word selected as the equivalent will itself have a range of meanings, at least some of which probably take the reader away from the Homeric. Significantly, Shewring omits Rieu from translators whose work he discusses. This omission perhaps reflects the tendency of much critical debate to concentrate on the translator's scholarly qualifications to address those key aspects of translation summarised by Shewring.

The most influential recent translations of Homer have been those produced by Richmond Lattimore (*Iliad* 1951, *Odyssey* 1965), Robert Fitzgerald (*Iliad* 1974, *Odyssey* 1961) and Robert Fagles (*Iliad* 1990, *Odyssey* 1996). Lattimore and Fitzgerald were professional classicists and university professors. Both translated a range of classical texts as well as Homer. Fagles co-operated closely with Bernard Knox, another university professor. They produced some joint translations and Knox wrote the lengthy and scholarly introductions to Fagles' translations of Homer. Also significant is the work of Michael Reck (*Iliad* 1994), which was strongly influenced by Milman Parry's research into the oral origins of epic and was intended for the spoken voice. Reck was also influenced by Ezra Pound's definition of literature as 'news that stays news' – a poet's equivalent of Silk's notion of 'immediacy' in Homer.[5]

Surveys of college lecturers in the USA have revealed that in the 1980s Lattimore's *Iliad* was the preferred translation of more than three-quarters of respondents, with Fitzgerald's a distant second.[6] Lattimore's translation was praised for 'beauty, readability, accuracy and faithfulness to the Homeric line'. Fitzgerald's *Iliad* was thought to be more impressionistic. However, Fitzgerald's *Odyssey* was preferred to Lattimore's, which had the same popularity rating as Rieu's prose version. Fitzgerald's *Odyssey* was singled out for its poetic quality. This praise was allied to the recognition that it was less literal than Lattimore's. A number of respondents also referred to the convenience of using a translation which was widely anthologised (for instance in *The Norton Anthology of World Masterpieces*). The survey revealed that attempts to choose translations for college use had to resolve the sometimes conflicting criteria of closeness to the form and vocabulary of the Greek with the desire for independent poetic quality and readability.

These criteria also dominate translation criticism by professional scholars. Much has been made of the fact that Lattimore has published his own poetry, as well as being a classical scholar, although few critics regard his translations as poetic in their own right. It has been suggested that, while his work provides the closest guide to the Greek, it can appear leaden and stilted to the reader. Yet it has also been praised for revealing to readers those aspects of the Homeric poems which have been judged most important by modern professional scholars. Certainly it is these lexical and scholarly attributes which underlie the praise of Lattimore given by Hugh Lloyd-Jones.[7] Although Lloyd-Jones praises Lattimore as both a scholar and a poet, his analysis of Lattimore's translations is primarily based on comparison with other translations and not on evaluation as poetry: 'It seems to me that he has done better with nobility, as well as with accuracy, than any other modern verse translator'. Lloyd-Jones also praises Lattimore's determination to avoid 'mistranslation' in the sense that he did not use his own preferred word but instead used the word which translated the Greek. In contrast, Lloyd-Jones attributed the success of Rieu's translations from the Greek to his ability to communicate a good plot in a clear and readable way, rather like the writer of a good detective story.[8] Rieu's *Odyssey* is less charitably described as a 'Trollopian travesty'.[9]

It has to be said that it is not only non-scholars who have been accused of 'mis-translation'. In the early twentieth century Gilbert Murray, Professor of Greek at Glasgow University at the age of twenty-three and later Regius Professor of Greek at Oxford, said in his first Presidential Address to the Classical Association, 'The Scholar's special duty is to turn the written signs in which old poetry or philosophy is now enshrined back into living thought or feeling. He [*sic*] must so understand as to relive.' At the time this was a revolutionary doctrine, as serious scholarship was mainly concerned with textual studies. Murray's verse translations, epecially of Euripides and Aristophanes, also involved him in close contacts with figures in the theatre, such as Granville Barker, Sybil Thorndike and George Bernard Shaw, who caricatured him in *Major Barbara* but also said that Murray's translations had the impulsive power of original works. They sold nearly 400,000 copies, although his critics said that, in the process of 'reliving', some qualities of the original vanished to be replaced by others which the original possessed only remotely or not at all.[10]

Translations of Latin epic have provoked similar disputes. David West, who is both a professional scholar and a translator, has tried to bridge the false dichotomy between scholarship and poetry, pointing out when discussing the *Aeneid* that ideally a translator 'should honour the drama, the characterisation and the details'. The 'details', he said, included poetic resources such as sound effects, pauses within the line, and the subtle effects of Latin word-order. West also gives an emphatic gloss on the meaning of the word 'accurate': 'an accurate translation which has none of the eloquence and poetic power of the original has committed the most heinous of all possible inaccuracies'.[11] West's stated aim in his own translation of Vergil was to be loyal to both the spirit and the letter of the original – 'I have tried to be utterly faithful to everything I see and hear in the Latin, the rhetoric, nuances, colour, tone, pace, passion, even the peerless music of Virgil's verse.' He believes that in order to produce readable English which honours the richness of Vergil's language, a translator has sometimes to search for the right English words at the expense of Latin idiom.[12] In stating this aim the poetic integrity of the new work is given equal status with the scholarship of the translator. For this reason West praises the 'eloquence and fire' of Douglas' translation into Scots.

The approach of scholar-translators such as West echoes the aim of Dryden and is more broadly summed up in D.S. Carne-Ross's claim (1961) that translation involves 'the recreation in a new language by whatever means are open to the translator of an equivalent beauty, an equivalent power, an equivalent truth'.[13] This approach suggests that it is an oversimplification to see scholarly and poetic aims as *necessarily* opposed. Although they may sometimes conflict in practice they can be brought together as part of a cultural process.

Clearly, then, there are several levels of activity and of response to the processes involved in translation. It is not possible simply to translate one word by its apparent verbal equivalent; the 'letter' is not enough. There is a complex web of tone, register and meaning which draws on the effects of vocabulary, sound, rhythm and metre in both the source text and the translation. This web is also shaped by the fact that translation is a movement which takes place not only across languages, but across time, place, beliefs and cultures. A translator's aim to communicate the 'nobility' of Homer or the 'sublimity' of Vergil is not a matter of simple lexical transfer but of cultural shaping and interpretation. It is a commonplace to say that something is lost in all translations. However, asking precisely what is lost in a particular work, and comparing this with what is gained, makes for a far more interesting inquiry. In different kinds of translations, different versions of the balance sheet emerge. Dryden, for instance, distinguished between metaphrase, paraphrase and imitation. Metaphrase involved a word-by-word and line-by-line transition into the new language. Paraphrase followed the sense of the original rather than the words; the sense might be amplified but not changed. Imitation signified a greater distance from the original in both words and sense; the translator came closer to creating a new work. Both Dryden and Denham (1615-69) stressed this aspect of 'poetry into poetry' describing it as 'transfusion'.

Recognition of the importance of the different kinds of translational relationship for both transmission of the power of the source text and for generating new poetic energy surely underlies the recent popularity of anthologies of poetic responses to Homer, Vergil, Horace and Ovid (such as *Homer in English* 1996, *After Ovid* 1994). These selections demonstrate the creative relationship between the classical texts and the work of individual authors and poetic movements. Critical debate now stresses the importance of looking at a version or imitation of an ancient text in the context of the modern writer's whole work, and this applies equally whether the translator is a professional scholar, a poet or a hybrid figure. This, together with the impact of modern literary criticism and increased awareness that meaning is not fixed or determined but constructed, negotiated and provisional, means that translations can be more readily accepted into the community of debate about meaning, rather than sidelined within the narrow framework of judgements about lexical accuracy and 'fidelity'.

The critical reception of Seamus Heaney's translation of the Anglo-Saxon epic *Beowulf* graphically illustrates the multi-layered debate. In his introduction to the work, Heaney writes of the way in which, once a poem is generally read in translation in university and college courses, it comes to be associated with a certain kind of authority, as though written on what Osip Mandelstam in discussing Dante called 'official paper'. Heaney asserts that, on the contrary, a work of 'imaginative vitality' possesses its own continuous present, although its narrative may belong to an earlier time.[14] In discussing his approach to translation Heaney acknowledges the importance of scholarship, and his account of the impact of academic studies of *Beowulf* on its modern poetic treatment in many ways parallels the influence on recent translations of Homer of scholarly studies of time, place, language and structure in Greek epic.

Despite acknowledging the laborious line-by-line work involved in the early stages, Heaney tends in practice to use the words translation and version interchangeably. As a poet, his interest is in the migration of language and ways of balancing the 'old and strange' with the 'shock of the new', but response to his translation has included criticism of his use of words of Irish origin and of the modern political resonances in his work. For example, in discussing his choice of words, Heaney describes his excitement at discovering a link between the Ulster Irish word 'thole' and the Old English word meaning 'to suffer'. He also justifies his use of the word 'bawn' to refer to a keep. 'Bawn', derived from the Irish word for a fort for cattle, became in Elizabethan English a fortified building used by the English planters in Ireland to keep the indigenous population away. The leap between the first kind of linguistic migration to the second was too much for some scholars, particularly since Heaney's work was initially commissioned by the Norton Anthology and could have become precisely the kind of influential university text (on 'official paper', no doubt) that Lattimore created for Homer. Heaney's translation was in the event awarded the 1999 Whitbread Book of the Year award, despite some residual debate about whether a translation really qualified as a new work. The Chairman of the Judges commented: 'This was a master poet breathing life into a great work of art which has only been known to a small number of academics. He has retrieved a buried golden treasure.'[15]

The idea of retrieving buried treasure, with its nostalgic undertones, certainly underplays the social and political impact that a translation can make. Heaney's subversive insertion of the word 'bawn' has already been noted. The use of classical texts and references as masks for political criticism has a long history. For instance, in 1649 Christopher Ware wrote a translation of Sophocles' *Electra* which drew parallels between the House of Atreus and the deposed House of Stuart, with its executed king. Given the brutal history of the House of Atreus, the analogy is something of a two-edged sword, but the implication was certainly that an avenging Orestes might be needed.

Quite apart from demanding that the writer convey the richness of ambiguity that energises the source plays themselves, translations of Greek drama present special problems. Some translations are created primarily to be read on the page, other translators aim at least at 'speakability' or, more ambitiously, at performability. Modern approaches to the study of Greek drama now give performance equal status with text. This has affected both the approaches to the translation of the text and the performance on the stage. As with translation of epic, it has become almost a convention that theatre practitioners consult and take advice from professional classicists, sometimes about staging and the conventions within which the Greek play was created, sometimes about translation and script, more often about both. Recent examples include Oliver Taplin as advisor to the Royal National Theatre production of Aeschylus' *Oresteia* as translated by Ted Hughes (1999), and in a different vein, Margaret Williamson's work with Timberlake Wertenbaker on the translation of the three Sophocles plays performed in sequence as *The Thebans* by the Royal Shakespeare Company (1991, published text 1992). It might almost be said that academic advisors perform the role of cultural gate-keepers.

When meaning is transmitted through the medium of a stage performance, words are not the sole or even necessarily the most important vehicle of translation. Every aspect of the staging – set, design, lighting, costume, music, physical movement including body language, gesture and choreography – is part of the process of interaction with the audience, and thus is part of the translation. When subjected to analysis, these aspects of the production provide a kind of commentary, both on the ways in which the director, designer and actors have interpreted the play and also on how they see its relationship with the receiving cultures, in which the members of audiences are situated and out of which they respond. Debates about staging and about the non-verbal translational processes involved, often centre on issues of 'authenticity' or of 'contemporisation' which parallel the debates about accuracy, poetic equivalence and mistranslation which surround printed translations.

The ways in which different kinds of 'translators' embed their commentary in their finished work are, of course, many and varied. Few poets are as direct as Gavin Douglas, who exploited the medieval convention of the Prologue, although it is significant that Heaney included marginal comments in his version of *Beowulf* because of the readers' probable unfamiliarity with the names, the story and the concepts. Some scholars working in translation studies have urged translators to emerge from the cloak of invisibility and to reveal, even flaunt, their presence in footnotes. There have been some interesting developments in this technique, notably by Josephine Balmer who has moved from restricting footnotes to mythological or historical explanations towards footnotes which comment on the process of translation in relation to the particular strategies of the source text. Her aim, she has stated, is 'to help monolingual as well as bilingual readers, to give them the experience of comparison, of judgement more normally reserved for the scholar'.[16]

This raises important questions about the way in which the translator copes with the range of levels of familiarity with the source which the reader, listener or spectator may have. At one level is the receiver who is familiar with both the language and the cultural context of the source. Here, nuances in the way in which equivalence is communicated or difference suggested are a key element in response. Some receivers may not know the ancient language but have knowledge of the source culture. Others may know the 'story', the outline of a myth, or recognise a famous name such as 'Odysseus' or 'Antigone'. Some may have second-hand stereotypical views about gods and heroes; others know nothing, and in these cases the strategies which the writer/director adopts to inform understanding are an important aspect of translational techniques.

Debate about these techniques is by no means confined to classicists and literary and theatre criticics. In recent years Translation Studies has developed as an area of specialist research and study. There have been important studies of the manipulative aspects of translation (Hermans, 1985; Lefevre, 1992). However, most of the discussion of translations from Greek and Latin has been confined to historical studies (from Kelly, 1979 to Venuti, 1995) or to descriptive surveys (Bassnett-McGuire, 1980) with some attempt to adapt purely descriptive models to focus more on the interaction between source and target languages and cultures (Toury, 1995). Interest in translation of Greek plays (stimulated by Arrowsmith and Shattuck, 1961) has been extended and refreshed by recent journal articles and published interviews with translators. The historical, moral and political role of translations in the construction and reshaping of cultural identities, including gender, is now an important aspect of broader cultural studies (for example Cronin, 1996; Simon, 1996). The role of classical referents and source texts in this process is significant and will be discussed in Chapters 5 and 6. Furthermore, the concept 'translation' often functions as a metaphor for a whole web of cultural activities. This means that the critical debate about the merits of different kinds of translation covers a wide range of issues, some openly acknowledged and others less so. Debates about scholarship, interpretation and the relationship between lexical and poetic equivalence, about the relationship between scholars, poets and theatrical practitioners, and about the receiving communities of readers, listeners and spectators raise large questions about the cultural origins, migration and 'ownership' of ancient poetic and dramatic works and about power structures in both ancient and modern societies. All these questions were in various ways present in the extracts from debates about translations of canonical texts quoted earlier in this chapter.

The enlargement in understanding and analysis of the conceptual scope of the term 'translation' is shown by the shift from the rather narrow hierarchic implications of criteria such as 'fidelity' towards notions of 'equivalence'. It is also represented by renewed acceptance of the crucial relationship between translations and new works, by a recognition of the relationship between translation activities and a writer's work as a whole, and by a growing awareness that 'equivalence' embraces difference as well as similarities. The importance of shifts in translational norms *within* cultures, that is in perceptions about what constitutes a translation and about how it might be judged (Hermans, 1991, 1996) has resulted from recognition of the importance of ideological frameworks, patronage, patterns of language and meaning, and from the shifting relationships between central texts and the processes of cultural change.

The chapters which follow focus on these shifts in translational norms, concentrating especially on examples which challenge fixed or monolithic assumptions about the relationship between ancient texts and their modern communication and realisation. They explore how various kinds of translation interact with the dynamics of cultural transmission and cultural change. The aim will be to examine ways in which shifts in translational norms map onto broader aspects of cultural change. Thus the very phrase 'translating cultures' is multi-layered. It suggests, at one level, that translating words also involves translating or transplanting into the receiving culture the cultural framework within which an ancient text is embedded. Futhermore, different cultures (and sub-cultures such as those represented by the artist, the politician, the academic, the theatre practitioner and the readers and audience) may create and enact their own translational norms, so in that sense translation is an activity which enables movement across boundaries. At a deeper level, the phrase suggests that cultures are actually created and defined by various kinds of translation.

2

Reverence and Subversion in Nineteenth-Century Translation

Ease is my plague: ease makes thee void
Catullus, with these vacant hours,
And wanton: ease that hath destroyed
Great kings, and states with all their powers.
W.E. Gladstone, 'Catullus to Lesbia', *Carmina* 51,
in *Translations by Lord Lyttleton and the
Rt. Hon. W.E. Gladstone* (1861)

It used to be thought that the nineteenth century represented a dark void in the relationship between classical poetry and translation into English. This view is based on the belief that there have been two golden ages in the relationship between classical poetry and English versions of them, the first running from the mid-sixteenth (Surrey, Golding and Chapman) to the mid-eighteenth century (Pope, Johnson) and the second developing in the twentieth century. The Romantics and Victorians were seen as handicapped by the authority and respect in which classical culture was held in the nineteenth century, an authority which inhibited them from engaging on terms of equality with Greek and Roman sources. Although there has been increasing recognition of the importance of exceptions to this generalisation, some of the cultural and aesthetic judgements associated with it have persisted. Even the editors of the wide-ranging anthology, *The Oxford Book of Classical Verse in Translation* (Poole and Maule, 1995), have suggested that nineteenth-century writers were 'cowed by the supposed authority of the classics', that 'far too many nineteenth-century translations are written on their knees, as it were' (p. xlv) and that it was only later that Pound and the modernists would not 'have anything to do with this cripplingly reverential position'.

I do not think that nineteenth-century practice and attitudes to translating classical texts were either as unified or as sterile as such traditional judgements suggest. On the contrary, the variety of approaches to translation and the broadening spectrum of authorship in the nineteenth century offer evidence of fierce debate, not only about the nature and purposes of translation and its cultural and political implications, but also about the role of translation in the lives and work of writers and in the perceptions of both the classically educated and the broader readership.

This chapter first describes general trends and then examines the contribution of some individual translators who foreshadow the cultural and aesthetic changes that underpin the sometimes startling twentieth-century refigurations of classical poetry and drama. Attitudes to and reworking of the literature and art of the ancient world not only represent a significant strand in nineteenth-century social and cultural history, they also provide an index for the analysis of change in scholarly, educational and artistic conventions (see Gilmour, 1993; Jenkyns, 1980; Stray, 1998; Turner, 1981, 1982). The question of initial access to classical learning and the use to which it might subsequently be put reveals important areas of gender and class exclusion and also highlights challenges to and complicity with dominant cultural and political power structures. Competition to appropriate and control the classical canon, including translation, made classical texts part of the battlefield of social change. The awareness that assumptions about meaning and influence derived from the classical tradition and its literature were actively being contested was intensified by the shift in interest in the early nineteenth century from Rome to Greece.

At the end of the eighteenth century, perceptions of Rome had been focussed on the (supposed) moral and political rectitude of the values of the Roman Republic. This implied a strictly ordered hierarchy underpinned by the dedication of the élite to a 'class' solidarity which they saw as congruent with service to the state. Subsequently, the Bonapartists exploited the imagery associated with Roman imperial power. The struggle for Greek independence from the Turks in the early nineteenth century produced two important changes in perception. Not only was there a greater interest in Greece (fanned by the writing and political activities of Shelley and Byron) but, even more important, there was an increased realisation that the implications of ancient culture might be double-edged. Greek culture, like Roman, could be reconstructed as a model of élite taste, but it also (in contrast to the most commonly read Roman authors) contained ideas which could encourage radical political debate, social reform and even some aspects of democracy. In addition, the role of the gods in epic, lyric and drama could be seen as challenging to many aspects of Christian monotheism, and the stress on the emotions of the individual and on tensions in the relationship between individual, family and society, had resonances for inquiring aspirational minds in Romantic and Victorian society.

Knowledge of the ancient Greek language was never as well established as that of Latin, even among the élite, so the expansion of interest in Greek history and literature led to a very substantial increase in translations, suggesting that both translators and readers were inspired to want more. In the 1820s the number of published translations from original texts rose to fifty-five from a base figure of eighteen in the previous decade, and later on, in the 1860s, there was a further increase, probably based on the needs of school and university students.

Taking translations of Homer into English as an example, it is possible to identify some distinct changes in the genesis and direction of translational practices. In general, the backgrounds of those producing translations became much wider, and there were more opportunities for those outside the traditional aristocratic or scholarly fields to publish their work. In the nineteenth century translations were produced, often for publication, by clerics, politicians, poets, scholars and people seeking change or stimulation in a field contrasting with that of their daily business occupation. A list of authors of a selection of translations looks very different from that of a list of classical scholars of the time. There was also a significant increase in the importance of published work by female translators.

In the first half of the nineteenth century, translation of epic into English was heavily influenced by the earlier translations of Chapman, Dryden, Pope and Cowper. The status of translation as itself a literary and autonomous work was recognised by the publication of *A Classical Manual* (1827, 1833), with mythological, historical and geographical commentary on Pope's *Iliad* and Dryden's *Aeneid*, as well as by various commentaries which related a particular version to discussion of the practical purposes of the text itself (for example, published under the pseudonym 'Ou Tis', on Cowper's version of *The Odyssey of Homer*, 1843). Gradually, however, awareness of 'the Homeric question' (or controversy) began to seep through from German scholarship and mingled with ideas already familiar to British and Irish readers from Robert Wood's *Essay on the Original Genius and Writings of Homer* (1761, published 1775). Issues concerning single or multiple 'authorship' in Homeric epic, the chronology and relationship between oral tradition and writing and the degree of historicity attributed to Homeric society, all began to affect translators' approaches. By the middle of the century translations were increasingly seen to take a stance on details of orality and composition. This affected verse and prose rhythms and choice of language and form, as well as decisions to emphasise either 'mythological' or 'realist' interpretations of Homer.

Prefaces to nineteenth-century translations frequently allude to the writers' aims to recreate 'faithfully', 'literally' or even 'for the English' (*Homer for the English, Iliad V*, London and Eton 1860). However, in practice notions of faithfulness or equivalence varied. There were sometimes disparities between the demands of scholarship which was rooted in the source language and the translator's sense of the target readership's social and moral values and attitudes (and of their aesthetic and educational capabilities). One aspect of this problem is evident in the difficulties over verse form. The Greek hexameter does not easily transfer into English metre. Matthew Arnold was among those who judged that an English hexameter could be produced and would communicate Homer's effect, and many translators attempted this. However, translations into blank verse were also popular, and some experimented with Spencerian stanzas. Towards the end of the century, prose became more influential (Butcher and Lang, *The Odyssey*, 1879).

Just as significant were experiments in using popular metres and ballad forms to try to recreate the original conditions of the Homeric oral tradition in which the poems were thought to have been heard by popular audiences. Those attempts varied from the vigorous to the comic; for example, William McGinn's *Homeric Ballads* was serialised in Fraser's magazine (1838 onwards) and although praised by Matthew Arnold and by Gladstone was thought by other critics to verge on parody: 'There was Argus stretched, his flesh all filled with the dog-worrying flea' (McGinn, *Odyssey* XVII, *The Dog Argus*, Stanza 5). There was even a burlesque translation of the *Iliad*, based on a late eighteenth-century version (4th edition 1797) and sufficiently popular to warrant further editions in New York (1809) and Philadelphia (1889), although it had incurred the wrath of the father of the supposed author, T. Bridges.

There were, however, few attempts to create stage versions of Homer, although theatre burlesque was important in popular culture and Homeric themes were mediated via Greek tragedy in works such as Reece's *Agamemnon and Cassandra: or the Prophet and Loss of Troy* (Prince of Wales Theatre, Liverpool, 1868). Burlesques based on Greek tragedy included *Agamemnon at Home; or, The Latest Particulars of that Little Affair at Mycenae* (1867) and a considerable number based on Euripides' *Medea*. There was also at least one written burlesque of a Greek tragedy, the anonymously authored *The Chinaid; or, The Persae of Aeschylus Burlesqued* (Oxford, 1843). Some burlesque productions incorporated a high degree of mythological allusion, while *Arion; or, the Story of Lyre* (1872) included jokes, the appreciation of which required a knowledge of Greek epic formulae (discussed by E. Hall, 1999). The author, F.C. Burnand, was an associate of W.S. Gilbert. Having struggled with Latin and Greek, at Eton he claimed to have created a burlesque of Vergil (*Dido*, 1860) in order to take revenge on the classics.

This degree of translational sophistication suggests that the transplantation of epic and drama into popular culture was achieved at a number of levels. Popularisation was evidently commercially successful. It could also involve self-conscious metatheatre, that is allusion to translations and stagings which were created as part of 'high culture'. A good example is Edward Leman Blanchard's burlesque of Sophocles *Antigone* (1845). Blanchard's work, *Antigone Travestre*, used for the set an imitation of the large booth portable theatre with interior stage which was a vital means of taking theatre outside London and bringing it to a wider audience (Hall, 1999). In this way it was to subvert the archaeologically serious but in some way unintentionally comic effects of the Covent Garden *Antigone*, which was based on a German production involving careful translation from the Greek, supervised by a noted classical scholar from Berlin University and then translated again from German into English under the title *An Imitative Version of Sophocles' Antigone, with its Melo-Dramatic Dialogue and Choruses, as Written and Adapted to the Music of Dr. Felix Mendelssohn Bartholdy by W. Bartholomew* (London 1845). The production aimed at authenticity in costume and set. Apparently, however, the chorus of sixty was not properly rehearsed and was lampooned in a *Punch* cartoon. The Covent Garden production also inserted a ballet sequence, to appeal to current taste, in which it was evidently successful since it ran for forty-five performances in London and was then staged in Edinburgh and Dublin, although the actor William Macready described it as 'low, provincial rant and extravagant pantomime' and wrote that if it was a true representation, then the Athenians must have had very poor taste.[1]

So it is clear that both the staging of plays and burlesques and the increase in written translations raised acute questions about the relationship between ancient and modern not only in terms of the classical aspects of language itself but in respect of aesthetic, moral, political and social values. In 1840 the Irish nationalist Thomas Davis in an address to the Historical Society at Trinity College Dublin described classical texts as 'shafts into the richest mines of thought which time has deposited'. However, he deplored the practice of concentrating on learning the ancient languages and considered that a good translation would communicate most of the meaning. In his view, it was that aspect of classical culture which was vital for Irish people's sense of history and identity. Translation was almost a conventional occupation for senior statesmen and prelates including Gladstone, Derby and Lord John Russell. Gladstone wrote extensively on key questions in Homeric scholarship, likening Homer to 'a remedial specific [which] by contact with the truth and strength of nature, should both improve its vigilance against deceit and danger and increase its vigour and resolution for the discharge of duty'.[2]

There was, however, fierce debate on the desirability or otherwise of the kind of model which Homer provided. The academic and translator Blackie thought the undemocratic Homer a useful counterweight to liberal values. Some Christians managed to fit pagan Greek religion and morality into a system of progress and divine revelation; others were disturbed by it. The cultural function of Homer among the ancient Greeks was thought to parallel that of the Bible in nineteenth-century European culture, and the theological and critical issues raised were sufficiently acute for the suitability of Homer for the syllabus at Oxford University to be challenged in the 1850s. Nevertheless, Greek literature and especially Homer held a significant place in educational requirements (including university matriculation, home and Indian civil service and army examination requirements) for there to be a proliferation of students' manuals, literal translations with parsing, interpaged and interlinear versions, summaries and paraphrases. These types of works were in demand by examination candidates and suggest that depth of knowledge in the ancient languages was less secure than is sometimes imagined.

In the middle of the century, there was an intense debate between F.W. Newman (brother of the Cardinal) and Matthew Arnold about the nature and purpose of translation. Arnold was by this time withdrawing from creative work, disturbed especially by the implications of his own profound sense of unease and despair expressed in his poem 'Empedocles on Etna', which was first published in 1852 and then withdrawn. Newman's edition and translation of the *Iliad* (1856) was based on his view that to be 'faithful' a translation should affect the reader just as the original affected its ancient audience, retaining every peculiarity especially if the original had included concepts and expressions distant from the norms of the society of the creating poet. So in order to represent this sense of distance in his own language and culture, Newman deliberately archaised, using alliteration, rhythms and words derived from Anglo-Saxon poetry. Arnold strongly criticised Newman in his Oxford Lectures *On Translating Homer* (1860-61). He argued that Homer's poetry was rapid, plain, direct and noble and that Newman's translation was 'odd' and 'ignoble' resulting from a false analogy between Homer and popular ballads. The furore led to a rash of journal and magazine essays on translation and to a further increase in publication of translations. The underlying conflict between the approaches of Arnold and Newman was about whether translations should, or could, seek to 'universalise' meaning and remove cultural differences. The dispute provided a wider perspective on the continuing debate about how to convey the style and spirit of the original while remaining 'faithful' to the letter, that is to its form and constructions.

An article by Robert Tyrell on 'Translation as a fine art' shows how slowly overt awareness of the changes in approach was disseminated.[3] Published in 1887, Tyrell's article began by claiming:

> The future historian of scholarship in England will point to the last twenty years or so as the epoch when translation first began to be cultivated as an art. Of course this is due in no small measure to the fact that till quite lately commentaries on the ancient writers were nearly always in Latin. But for some time after English commentaries became the rule, it was customary to make translation a mere vehicle for the elucidation of the construction. Commentators absolutely neglected all attempts to reproduce the style and spirit of the original. Students, on making their first acquaintance with the masterpieces of Greek and Latin poetry, could not help regarding Sophocles and Virgil as bald, frigid and stilted.

Tyrell went on to praise the translations of Sophocles produced by Professor Jebb as 'really genuine poetry ... [they] bring the English reader as near to Sophocles as he can possibly hope to come without acquiring a knowledge of the language in which Sophocles wrote'.

It is clear from the remainder of the article that Tyrell was concerned with the question of the relationship between classical and English literature, by that time a crucial debate in education. Tyrell thought that Jebb's translations reflected 'a long and loving study of English literature' and actually offered better equivalence to the Greek than a more literal version which might actually miss the meaning – 'a good translation is often the best comment. Half a page of talk about the meaning of a passage does not tell so much as one line of perfect rendering'. This approach seems very close to describing translation as the creation of a dialogue between the classical and English literary traditions. This adds one more dimension to the 'field of engagement' between ancient and modern, joining the issues of scholarly enquiry, social and educational contexts and contrasting perceptions of the relationship between ancient and modern thought and religion which have framed the translational activities discussed so far in this chapter. To these might now be added recognition of the capacity of translation to generate other creative work (via the transplantation of classical allusion, images and themes), which is either directly literary or with a wider cultural focus.

Thus the picture which emerges is that of translation contexts which were not only varied but which changed at different rates in different spheres. This can be illustrated by looking at the work of three women writers who each demonstrated different kinds of empowerment based on the increasing diversity of translational practices.

> It was not entirely out of devotion to her future husband that she wished to know Latin and Greek. Those provinces of masculine knowledge seemed to her a standing-ground from which all truth could be seen more truly.
>
> *Middlemarch*, book 1, ch. 7

Thus George Eliot describes the innermost thoughts of her heroine Dorothea Brooke. In the event Dorothea found the role of helpmate to her boring husband intellectually as well as emotionally constraining, and while Eliot's omniscient narrative voice conveys the gendered conception of knowledge which was associated with classical learning, the very certainty of the words gives an ironic hint of the inadequacy of that perception. Yet for most aspects of nineteenth-century life the basic facts of the statement were true. Women's access to Latin and Greek was limited by restrictions on education and opportunity. It therefore followed that the knowledge and insights afforded by the ancient languages were seen as 'masculine'. Most women who learned Latin and Greek did so in order to assist the education or research of brothers, sons or husbands, and in general the translation activities of women (in whatever language) were justified in similar terms, with the possible additional function of augmenting the family income by undertaking routine hack work.

Women who rebelled against these norms risked masculine displeasure, especially if they did so publicly. Elizabeth Barrett (1806-61), for example, was indulged by her father in her youth in the printing of her epic poem *The Battle of Marathon*, but when she published her translation of Aeschylus' *Prometheus Bound* (1833) the critics were savage and she withdrew it from circulation. One described it as 'a daring enterprise for a young lady and one which could not have been

attempted without a degree of learning highly creditable to her indus-
try and perseverance [... but] not a very successful one'.[4] Another
commented that Barrett's 'genius, utterly unaided by art [is] continu-
ally running wild ... but where scholars cannot agree, ladies may be
excused mistranslating'.[5] Barrett was so devastated that she published no more translations of whole Greek works. Instead she reworked
her version of the *Prometheus* and wove the imagery into her correspondence with Robert Browning, describing herself as bound by
paternal authority as if she were Prometheus 'taking up my chain
again and acquiescing in this hard necessity'.[6]

Browning responded in Promethean language – 'I stand by and see
the infliction of tyranny on the unresisting'. Browning's close examination of Barrett's translation and his comparisons with the Greek
text chart the growing intimacy of their correspondence. This is especially so in their discussion of how best to render in English Aeschylus'
celebration of the hopes (yearnings, longings, desires) which
Prometheus gave to humans with the gift of fire. Eventually the two
writers saw Mr Barrett as 'father Zeus with his paternal epistles and
peggings to the rock'. The correspondence suggests that Elizabeth
Barrett saw her translation work and its reception by critics as emblematic of the restriction she suffered in her personal life.
Significantly, her revised translation was published in *Poems* (1850),
which included the sequence of love poems masquerading under the
title *Sonnets from the Portuguese* which in early editions is included in
the section entitled 'Translations'. This suggests that translation, in
its various guises, provided a means by which she could mask her
exploration and expression of her own emotions and sexuality.

A very different set of problems was encountered by Anna Swanwick
(1813-99). She was the daughter of a prosperous Liverpool merchant
and deeply influenced by her family's liberal and Unitarian ethos
which held that it was necessary for both men and women to develop
intellectual powers in order to foster their religious and moral capaci-
ties. She was dissatisfied with her school education, which included
neither Mathematics nor Latin nor Greek (see further Hardwick,
2000a). Many years later she said to women students at Bedford
College London (which she was instrumental in founding), 'I often
longed to assume the costume of a boy in order to learn Latin, Greek

and Mathematics, which were then regarded as essential to a liberal education for boys but were not thought of for girls'.[7]

Swanwick studied German with her sister and then visited Germany to study both German and Greek, as she wished to read the New Testament in the original. While in Berlin, she began to translate the work of Plato into German. She had a private income, and her books resulted more from her scholarship and her wish to extend the availability of literature written in various languages than from any need to make a living. Her first publications were translations from Goethe and Schiller. She soon turned to translations from Greek tragedy, starting with *Prometheus Bound* and progressing to the *Oresteia* (1865) and the complete works of Aeschylus (1873, illustrated by Flaxman). Her translation of the *Oresteia* was very favourably reviewed, apart from some criticism of her use of blank verse for the iambics and rhyme for the lyrics. Among the letters of congratulation was one from W.E. Gladstone, who wrote to her as A. Swanwick, Esq. She replied, correcting him, and they became close associates. She was often the only woman, apart from Mrs Gladstone, present at his famous Thursday breakfasts, and recorded that they 'discussed Homer, Aeschylus, Dante, Shakespeare and Ireland'. One wonders whether they also discussed the question of women's suffrage, on which their views certainly differed. Swanwick became involved in the women's movement as a result of seeing how women campaigners were sometimes marginalised by their male colleagues in the movement against slavery. She signed the petition on suffrage organised by Barbara Bodichon and presented to Parliament by John Stuart Mill in 1866. Later she addressed public meetings as a respected 'elder' of the Suffrage movement.

Swanwick's translations from the Greek had two direct effects. First, together with her Introductions and general essays on classical and literary topics, they enabled people who did not know Greek to read the tragedies and so opened up knowledge of classical culture and especially of Athenian democracy. This aspect of her work was greatly praised by members of the Classical establishment such as Dr Butler of Trinity College, Cambridge, and Sir Richard Jebb (who admired her 'genuine sympathy with the original disciplined command of expression ... [and] fine literary tact'). Secondly, her work created new respect for women's scholarship. Even the notoriously patronising reviews in the most influential journals recognised the quality of her work and some specifically linked it to advancement of the cause of women's suffrage. The *Westminster Review* in 1865 even compared her translation favourably with that of male academics – 'the things that the reader may perhaps wonder to find in Blackie and not in her, are not in Aeschylus ... not only in tenderness, dignity, weight and in that masculine attribute terseness but also in understanding and intimate feeling of the Greek, the lady need not fear comparison with the Greek professor'.

Swanwick used the status achieved through recognition of her high standards of scholarship to advance various aspects of the women's movement. In addition to the suffrage, she campaigned for education at all levels for the poor and excluded. She started an evening school for poor girls at her London home in Woburn Square (venturing into the slums to recruit them, a habit she shared with Gladstone, although doubtless for different reasons). She supported the work of F.D. Maurice, Charles Kingsley and others in setting up working men's clubs and institutes, and her connection with Bedford College spanned fifty years. She attended classes ('to encourage the others'), acted as a chaperone and served on the College Council. She was active in the development of Somerville College, Oxford, and Girton College, Cambridge, insisting that the curriculum should be the same for both male and female students. She served on grant-awarding bodies for medical schools, teacher training colleges and women's halls.

The official history of Bedford College asserts that she was 'probably the most learned women associated with Bedford College at this time – was indeed one of the few learned women of the day. A Greek and Hebrew scholar, a devotee and translator of Goethe, she was dreaded in her world as a blue stocking.' The scholarly regard in which she was held gave authority to her practical work, and her translations are important evidence of the range of strategies adopted by Victorian Hellenists in mediating Greek values and religion to audiences in their own society. All her public work was informed by a high moral tone and this raises some significant issues for evaluation of her translations.

Swanwick's approach to translation into English on the one hand recognises her sense of the force of Greek political ideas concerning community and democracy, and on the other hand reflects her view that the Greeks, being pagans, could only be *progressing* towards a

34

fully Christian perception of religious and political morality. She thought that caution was needed in allowing the young to read Greek texts – 'the ancient classics, written by adults for adults, are beyond the intelligence of immature minds while in regard to the moral lessons to be drawn from them, the superiority in my opinion is vastly in favour of more modern writers'.[8] Her essays suggest that she regarded Homeric epic as particularly immoral, especially in respect of the behaviour of the gods and male heroes. She did not share the tendency of some Victorians, including Gladstone, to sanitise the brutality, exploitation and greed depicted in the poem.

When she chose to concentrate on Aeschylus, Swanwick was clearly in sympathy with the civic and democratic focus of the plays. She described her method of translation as having three main aspects. First, she acquired a detailed knowledge of the original, learning much by heart. Secondly, she aimed at accuracy. Thirdly, she tried to develop a metre as close to the original as the English language would permit, even at the expense of fluency. She approved of F.W. Newman's translation of the *Iliad* and rejected the 'domesticating' method of translation which emphasised fluency and easily assimilated dominant English cultural values into the translation. However, her attention was concentrated on the difference between 'domestication' and 'foreignisation' (or 'Newmanising', as Arnold called it) in matters of religion rather than in translation as such. She saw deviation from the original as a 'breach of trust', yet she was also disturbed by the fact that while Greek culture might in some respects be perceived as admirable (particularly in its fifth-century Athenian form), in religion it was pagan. She resolved this dilemma by arguing that religious ideas in Aeschylus marked a great stage in human progress, a prelude to Christianity, 'a dim but most wonderful foreshadowing' (Introduction to the *Oresteia*, p. xxviii). She thought translation should accommodate both fidelity to the original and a 'distancing' from nineteenth-century language and values and this is reflected in her choice of language for the translation of political terms; for instance she used the quasi-medieval 'liege' to represent *polis*-related terms. (Translating in the twentieth century, R.L. Lattimore used the term 'citizen'.) However, she occasionally lapses into a Christianised religious discourse, using words such as 'salvation', 'trespass' and 'sin' in the Greek Chorus's moral strictures concerning piety and duty to gods, parents and guests. In her translations Swanwick worked within the largely masculine norms accepted by scholarly progressive approaches to education and learning. She was a skilled networker. Men listened to her views because of her scholarly reputation, and the fact that she was a respected figure in the liberal 'establishment' added respectability to the causes she advocated and enabled her to play a significant role in improving educational opportunities for women.

Augusta Webster (1837-1894) was another distinguished woman translator whose work was acknowledged by critics to rank alongside that of Swanwick. Yet her background, lifestyle, prose style and literary work were very different. She studied Art and Modern Languages in Cambridge, Paris and Geneva, but her Greek was self-taught (initially to help a brother). As well as translations from the Greek her publications included novels, poetry, plays, essays and reviews (mainly in the *Athenaeum* and the *Examiner*). Her first collection of poems and her first novel were published under the pseudonym Cecil Hume (ambivalent as to gender; Swanwick had used the initial only of her first name). In 1863 the then Augusta Davies married Thomas Webster, a fellow of Trinity College, Cambridge, who became a solicitor in London. In 1866 she published her translation of Aeschylus' *Prometheus Bound* under her married name. The frontispiece credited Thomas Webster as editor. In contrast to their reception of Elizabeth Barrett's *Prometheus Bound*, the reviewers were full of praise – 'fidelity to the original without losing its spirit' (*Westminster Review*), 'done faithfully and conscientiously' (*Contemporary Review*), 'a certain poetic majesty ... discloses itself' (*Illustrated London News*). In 1868 she published her translation of Euripides' *Medea*, this time with no suggestion that she relied on her husband's editorship of the text. This translation was in verse and reviewers praised her close attention to the Greek text and her ability to render poetic equivalence.

Nevertheless the gendered and sometimes patronising languages of the reviews could sometimes produce comic effects. In 1868 an anonymous reviewer in the *Athenaeum* (probably J.M. Millard, Headmaster of Magdalen College School, Oxford) commented on Webster's translation of the *Medea* – 'the subject if not grand, is one of general interest ... it is also one which a lady might naturally be expected to handle with success as she must be able to enter fully into the feelings of the unfortunate heroine in her distressing condition'. (There is, incidentally, absolutely no evidence that Thomas Webster contemplated deserting his wife for a more politically advantageous alliance nor that Augusta Webster considered murdering her child.) Interest in the *Medea* may well have been stimulated by the Divorce Act of 1857. Certainly, new productions of the play followed soon after. Webster's translation was, however, a literary exercise, not created for the stage.

Like Swanwick's, Webster's authority as a translator also made her other work more influential. She was elected to the London School Board and campaigned for technical training and education for women. Her 'Essays on Suffrage' were published by the Women's Suffrage Union (1878), and a collection of her essays from the *Examiner* on the concerns of married women was reprinted as *A Housewife's Opinions* (1879). Her prose style was vigorous, unadorned and ironic. She described the current voting arrangements as 'the blind leading the dumb', supported Frances Cobbe's work for battered wives, ridiculed the opponents of women's suffrage and argued for accuracy in translation from an analogy with gin, which the Trades Descriptions Act decreed should be neat and not adulterated with sugar and water (*AHO*, p. 71).

Webster produced two essays on the subject of translation, and characteristically mocked some aspects of conventional norms. In a short essay, 'The Translation of Poetry' (*AHO*, pp. 61-5), she argued that the two opposing theories of translation ('the letter' and 'the spirit') were not mutually exclusive but interdependent. Her second and major essay on translation was 'A Transcript and a Transcription' (*AHO*, pp. 66-79). In it she compared and contrasted two translations of Aeschylus' *Agamemnon*. She criticised Morshead's translation as un-Aeschylean because it aimed to be flowing, literary and 'readable'. The other translation she analysed was by Robert Browning. She was an associate of the Browning circle and much influenced by some aspects of his poetry. She recognised the force of Browning's theory of translation, which she summarised as 'to be literal at every cost except that of violence to our language', but argued with caustic wit that his *Agamemnon* failed lamentably to meet that aim – 'the reader who knows no Greek at all will be left bewildered and incredulous ... without Aeschylus to translate Browning, how can they track out the meaning?' Her essay represented a serious challenge to the dominant

37

norm of the robust, terse and undecorated translation (qualities which were all considered masculine virtues). She claimed that for a good translation appreciation of the subtlety and allusiveness of Greek was not enough. Sensitivity to the equivalent qualities in English and the ability to communicate these was also required. Her skill lay in expressing these judgements in a literary style which was itself accepted as 'masculine and vigorous'. The further irony was that this essay was published alongside others such as 'Dull People', 'Husband Hunting', 'The Cost of a Leg of Mutton' and 'Parliamentary Franchise for Women Ratepayers'.

The most important aspect of Webster's approach to translation was her sense that a translation has a poetic identity of its own, which has to be able to excite the imagination and inform the understanding of the reader/audience in a way equivalent to that of the source text. When the relationship between her translations from the Greek and her own poetry is considered, it is evident that she needed both in order to give full reign to her concerns and her literary imagination. Combined with her scholarship, the directness of her insight and her imaginative sense led her to speculate about the perspectives and experiences of the female characters, which were either not directly represented or were completely excluded from the ancient texts and thus from contemporary readers' understanding. Although she did not use the word, her focus was on what modern scholarship would call 'silences'. In her work, she created a voice for the silenced in two ways. First, she wrote against the grain of convention, giving a vigorous and independent voice to the oppressed in her own society, notably in the central figure of the prostitute in her major work *A Castaway* (in *Portraits* 1870). Secondly, in the same volume, she used the form of the dramatic monologue to construct imagined responses from women in canonical Greek texts.

Circe and *Medea in Athens* use images of women to explore sexuality, revenge and the material and emotional realities of loneliness in ways that challenge the limits of both Greek and Victorian social conventions. They also show how, by comparing the new work or 'translation' with the source text, it is possible to discern the power of compulsory or voluntary cultural censorship, in both the ancient and modern traditions. In Homer, audience and reader response to the representation of the female figures is sometimes thought to have the

effect of creating complicity in the denigration of women, such as
Circe, who transgress the norms which ensure dependency. By contrast, Webster not only gives Circe a voice but leaves her in control of
the narrative and the emotions it creates. Ironically, by domesticating
Circe to the conventions of female emotions and Victorian ennui
Webster challenges both the stereotypical demonisation of Circe's
sexual powers and the reluctance of Victorian literature fully to
express female emotions. The opening lines subvert the conventional poetic representation of sunset to suggest the power of female
sexuality:

> The sun drops luridly into the west;
> darkness has raised her arms to draw him down
> before the time, not waiting as if wont
> till he has come to her behind the sea;

Then, in the second part of the poem, the voice of Circe addresses 'the
sickly sweet monotony', welcoming the storm which will disrupt 'this
long bright calm' and lead to the passionate relationship which she
desires. Circe combines contempt for the men who come to her with a
desperate longing for a fulfilling relationship. This effectively shifts
both moral and emotional aspects of gender relations and exposes the
double standard inherited from Homer and reaffirmed in the nineteenth century. The distance between classical texts and her own
present both allows and requires Webster to inhabit the dramatic
monologue form and to mask her own voice in that of Circe. In the
monologue *Medea in Athens* she deliberately transfers conventional
epithets across gender, most notably when the word 'ruined' with all
its contemporary associations, is transposed to the defeated and deheroised Jason, dead as the result of a blow from his ship's timbers.
He has been half-forgotten by Medea. What has survived is her sense
of betrayal and of triumph at her victory over him.

Although Webster's poetry was highly regarded by writer/critics
such as Christina Rossetti (who considered that like Elizabeth Barrett
Browning Webster combined 'masculine' and 'feminine' qualities in her
poetry), the late nineteenth century largely marginalised her work.
Gladstone excluded her from his list of poetesses, and the first edition
of A.H. Miles's anthology *The Poets and Poetry of the Nineteenth*

Century (10 vols, 1891-7) included only a few of her lyrics and none of her socially committed work. In more recent years her importance has begun to be recognised but there has been little direct understanding of the relationship between her translations and the rest of her work. This relationship is evident in her choice of issues, in the phrasing of her social and political essays, and in her creation in her dramatic monologues of the voices of female classical figures as a means to explore and challenge both ancient and modern gender norms. In so doing she also shifted the translational norms of her own time.

The *Medea* of Euripides is one of the most important ancient texts in mapping ways in which translational norms were treated, challenged and refigured. A further shift is evident in the work of Amy Levy (1861-89). Benefiting from improved educational opportunities for girls, she began to publish poetry from the age of thirteen and from 1876-9 studied classics while a pupil at Brighton and Hove High School for Girls. Unpublished manuscript letters written while she was at school testify to the level of classical activity there and speak of a fellow pupil working on a substantial translation from Ovid (see Hardwick, 2000b). From 1879 she was a student at Newnham College, Cambridge, for four terms and was the first Jewish student to be admitted. Her first volume of poems was *Xantippe [sic] and Other Poems* (1881). This is important for the title work, a striking dramatic monologue spoken by the wife of Socrates and giving voice to the distress and anger of Xanthippe because her desire for equality of esteem and intellectual parity with her husband and his circle was not taken seriously. The poem is very carefully placed in the literary-historical context of Plato's *Symposium* and exploits the form of the Platonic dialogue as a dramatic device. It both explicates and challenges the conventional verdict of history on Xanthippe (the shrewish wife who nagged the great Socrates).

Levy's next volume was *A Minor Poet and Other Verses* (1884). This contained a dramatised version of *Medea* in two scenes described as 'after Euripides'. Like *Xantippe*, it examines the physical and intellectual oppression of a confined woman. As the result of this treatment the women were driven either to symbolic expression of repressed violence (Xanthippe) or actual violence (Medea). Levy's treatment of Medea involved changes in focus, language and form which combine to anticipate later readings of the play. She introduced a new character, Nikias. There was no Chorus. This meant that direct social and moral commentary on the action was lacking. Instead she represented Nikias as an obnoxious social commentator, drawing out the Euripidean theme of barbarism and the rejection of aliens and expressing it in nineteenth-century idiom:

> I like not your swart skin and purple hair ...
> Give me gold hair, lithe limbs and gracious smiles
> And spare the strangeness.

In unmasking the sub-text in Euripides (analysed by recent scholarship: E. Hall, 1991), Levy also demonstrated the link with the overtly racist language and images in nineteenth-century literature and art (see Hardwick, 2000b). The tragedy was compounded by the fact that in Levy's work there was no refuge in Athens for Medea. Her final soliloquy is made as she leans on a rock, alone, outside the city, prostrated by its 'hissing hate'. A late nineteenth-century reader, aware of the contrasts with the source text, might be jolted into awareness of the contemporary implications. Levy adapted Euripides' dramatic form and vocabulary to challenge both Greek and modern constructions of gender and their associated behavioural norms. She also explored the racist implications of the Greek/barbarian polarity set out by Euripides. Her work recognised and critiqued a late nineteenth-century shift in the iconic status of Medea, no longer represented primarily as the wronged wife but as a violent outsider in whose construction gender and race stereotypes combine. In *Xantippe* we can hear something of Levy's own voice. In her *Medea* the monologue form was integrated into drama and both Greeks and Victorians unmasked.

The role of translation and related activities was crucial in developing nineteenth-century challenges to a variety of cultural norms – political, social, aesthetic. It deepened and refined awareness of the voices present in the source texts and enabled reconstruction of voices that were wholly or partly silenced. The writers who have been examined here vary greatly in their relationship to established conventions and in the directions in which they pushed the relationship between ancient texts and modern writing. Nevertheless, even those who wrote 'with the grain' rather than against it were far from reverent towards classical texts and culture. They variously recognised impiety, greed, brutality and oppression and used their knowledge to construct critiques of their own society. All refused to sanitise either ancient culture or their own. Webster and Levy began to redefine the relationship between the role of ancient culture in providing a mask behind which criticism and feeling could be expressed and its role in enabling a personal voice to develop and be heard. In so doing they also helped to bring about significant long-term changes in the norms and expectations which readers and critics brought to bear on translation.

3

The View from Translation:
Image, Window and Dissection

It was easy enough
to bend them to my wish
it was easy enough to
alter them with a touch
but you
adrift on the great sea,
how shall I call you back?
　　　　HD, 'Circe', *Hymen* (1921)

This chapter explores aspects of the relationship between translation
and the transplantation of classical images into new work. The writers
whose work is discussed all write across boundaries and challenge
norms – translational, cultural and aesthetic. The transitional mech-
nisms of the strategies they use reveal different emphases in the
relationship between source texts and modern poetry. In the case of
HD, who commented specifically on the role of ancient texts in her
creative writing and literary criticism, classical referents are seen as
images, condensing insights, and as windows, opening the way to
broader explorations. These aspects are given a distinctive focus in the
refiguration of ancient themes and images in twentieth-century war
poetry, where they generate expansion of awareness and transformation of sensibility. This process is radically inverted by Christopher
Logue, who constructs a window back into the *Iliad* in order to dissect
the epic's treatment of heroic values in the context of war.

HD (Hilda Doolittle, 1886-1961) was born and educated in the
United States. From 1911 she lived mainly in Europe. She was a
literary associate of Ezra Pound (who was also for a time her lover) but
subsequently married the editor, translator and writer Richard Ald-

43

ington. The marriage was not secure, and she went on to have a long-term relationship with Bryher (Winifred Ellerman) the novelist and modernist figure. In the 1930s she underwent psychotherapy, including analysis with Sigmund Freud.[1]

Along with Pound, HD was associated at the outset of her career with Imagism, a literary movement which tried to focus on the poetic communication of concentrated moments of experience, conveyed through techniques of concise expression, using concrete imagery and clear precision. Imagists experimented with verse forms, using short lyrically cadenced lines rather than regular metre. They shunned the abstract and avoided overt symbolism – Pound thought that 'the natural object is always the adequate symbol'.

HD subsequently moved into a much wider range of experimentation, including eventually dramatic verse and epic. Virtually all her work is permeated by her sense of the shaping role of classical texts.[2] Ancient poetry, especially Greek, was her starting point, and in her *Notes on Euripides, Pausanias and Greek Lyric Poets* (no date: the fourteen essays were probably begun in 1920) she described how, for her,

> The lines of this Greek poet [Euripides] (and all Greek poets if we have but the clue) are today as vivid and fresh as they ever were, but vivid and fresh not as literature (though they are that too) but as portals, as windows, ... I know that we need scholars to decipher and interpret the Greek, but that we also need poets and mystics and children to rediscover this Hellenic world, to see the words: the word being but the outline, the architectural structure of that door or window, through which we are all free, scholar and unlettered alike, to pass. We emerge from our restricted minds (with all due reverence to them of course) into a free, large, clear, vibrant, limitless realm, sky and sea and distant islands, and a shore line such as this in Egypt and another along the coast in Asia Minor or further towards the Bosphorus, and again Greece, Hellas, the thousand intimate bays, the foaming straits.[3]

HD was well read in classical literature, life and cultural history, although in terms of the categories she set out above she probably saw herself as a mystic rather than as a scholar, and her scholarship was sometimes derided by male critics such as T.S. Eliot. In fact, her poetry reveals deep knowledge not only of particular texts but of a whole range of poets and figures through whom she could address questions of female presence in classical literature. With her husband she was involved in the *Poets' Translation Series* (1915-16 and 1918-19) and produced translations and variations of the work of female poets – Sappho, Nossis, Anyte, Moero, Telesilla. She also drew on male poets such as Meleager, whom she saw as supporting women, and Euripides, who she thought raised important questions about female identity and experience. Her choice of texts is significant. She translated, transposed and rescued from obscurity poems in the Greek Anthology written by or about women. She translated Choruses from *Iphigenia at Aulis*, *Bacchae*, *Hippolytus* and all of *Ion*, into which she interwove her own comments. She produced her own version of *Hippolytus* and some shorter poems on female figures in epic (Circe, Calypso, Thetis, Helen, Cassandra). She developed the dramatic monologue to reinterpret myth from the viewpoint of the female figures, using changed narrative sequences and suggesting alternative ideological interpretations. The effect was to produce a critique of the canonical narrative and its conventional interpretation by critics and translators.

Eventually in the 1950s she composed a new epic, *Helen in Egypt* (1961). Here again her choice of subject is distinctive. In her autobiographical fictional work *Paint It Today* she had expressed her preference for the lyric over the epic, which she saw as dominated by the theme of war – 'she wanted the songs that cut like a swallow-wing the high untainted ether, not the tragic legions of set lines that fell like black armies with terrific force and mechanical set action, paralysing, or broke like a black sea to battle and to crush' (*PIT*, ch. 1, 13). In *Helen in Egypt* she drew on a wide range of contexts and perspectives on Helen, including the plays of Euripides, locating her within both maternal and erotic landscapes and using lyric monody to give voices to Helen and to her lovers Achilles, Paris and Theseus. She used choral sequences to weave together images from myth. In this way she subverted both epic form and narrative.

In challenging the norms associated with cultural transmission and the role of translation within it she also claimed to strike a blow for truth. She expressed this aim in her prose poem 'Helios and Athene'.

The serpent does not crouch at Athene's feet. The serpent lifts a
proud head under the shelter of her shield ...
Consider the birds. Be wise as serpents ...
Let daemons possess us! Let us terrify like Erynnes [*sic*], the
whole tribe of academic Grecians!

HD: Collected Poems 1912-1944

The allusion to the Furies suggests that HD saw herself as energising
ancient powers in revenge for what she saw as the appropriation and
sterilisation of ancient culture by the Academy.

Critical evaluation of HD's work, while recognising her classical
scholarship, used to emphasise the ways in which she used classical
authors to mask her exploration of themes of emotion and sexuality,
including lesbian orientation. However, the impact of 'personal voice'
theory has served to question this emphasis, and her use of Greek
myths and themes is increasingly seen to be a channel for her own
voice rather than just a dramatic mask. Comparison of successive
drafts of her poems suggests that this was beginning to happen as
early as 1916-17, possibly stimulated by her friendship with D.H.
Lawrence. Equally crucial in placing and evaluating her poetry is the
impact of her translation work, both within the texts of the poems and
during the writing process. For example, she translated a Chorus from
Euripides' *Hippolytus* (*Translations 1915-1920*) just before writing
'Phaedra' and the companion poems 'She Contrasts With Herself
Hippolyta' and 'She Rebukes Hippolyta' (*Hymen*, 1921). In 'She Rebukes Hippolyta' the language and values in Euripides are brought
into play with the more directly obvious influences from Swinburne's
and Pater's late nineteenth-century treatment of the theme. This is
evident in echoes of the frenzy associated with Artemis (in Euripides'
Hippolytus 215-22, 228-31):

> Hippolyta frail and wild
> galloping up the slope
> between great boulder and rock
> and group and cluster of rock.
> Was she so chaste,
> (I see it, sharp, this vision,
> and each fleck on the horse's flanks

46

of foam, and bridle and bit,
silver, and the straps,
wrought with their perfect art,
and the sun,
striking athwart the silverwork,
and the neck, strained forward, ears alert
and the head of a girl
flung back and her throat.)

HD's engagement with the Greek texts governs and disciplines within a formal framework her linking of images, personal commentary and the plurality of voices in the lyrics. The effect of her translation and of the refinement of translational techniques in her poetry is to add a new and challenging dimension to the transmission of classical texts. Because she keeps at the forefront of her experimentation some of the less frequently translated plays and authors, her work also serves to question narrow and monolithic conceptions of 'the classical'. Furthermore, her juxtaposition of images, perspectives and episodes relating to the same theme or figure but drawn from different authors anticipates poetic and dramatic techniques which developed later in the twentieth century.

HD rejected what she perceived as the masculinity and violence of much of Homeric epic. However, her gendered approach underestimated both the sensitivity of Homeric treatment of war and the sensibilities of male poets who refigured classical images in the light of their own personal experience and thereby also moved from behind a classical mask to allow the interplay of a range of voices including their own.

This process in action is highlighted in the work of male poets writing during the early part of the twentieth century in response to conflict in the First World War and in Ireland. Unlike HD, the male poets I shall discuss were not (with few exceptions) concerned with translation and commentary as such but were transplanting into their poetry ideas, images and situations from Greek and Roman poetry, especially Homer, and refining them in response to contemporary experience. Their translational techniques in various ways, some specific in their reference, some less so, reveal layers of meaning. The exploration of correspondences of situation and image with those in

Homer becomes a means of understanding the relationship between the world within a poem and the world outside. In some cases the effect is to redirect the reader's attention to the poetry of Homer, similarly rich and sometimes elusive in ranges of meaning (see Hardwick, 1992).

Homer was an especially fertile source of allusion for the poets of the First World War for a number of reasons. First, Greek texts were still part of the educational background of many middle- and upper-class young men. Secondly, ancient epic poetry and the *Iliad* in particular héld particular resonance because of its apparent stress on the role of the individual as hero, on his lasting fame (*kleos*) and on the glory brought by death in battle. Subsequent critics have termed this the 'good death', implying a death suffered with courage; a death which avoids the decline and indignities both of defeat and of the decrepitude of old age. Thirdly, there were geographical affinities between the situation of Troy on the coast of Asia Minor and the theatres of war, especially in the Gallipoli campaign of 1915.

Homeric referents were therefore an important means of developing the range of emotions and uncertainties on which the poets played. Far from reinforcing a simplistic view of heroism based on some unexamined appropriation or sanitisation of Homer, the most challenging poetry refigured images from ancient poetry in order to play on multiple layers of meaning and in so doing often subverted cultural norms. It is possible to see the beginnings of this process in a frequently anthologised poem by Patrick Shaw-Stewart, written during the Gallipoli campaign in 1915. The poet specifically compared his situation with that of Achilles:

> Achilles came to Troyland
> And I to Chersonese
> He turned from wrath to battle
> And I from three days' peace.
> Was it so hard, Achilles,
> So very hard to die?
> ... Stand in the trench Achilles,
> Flame-capped, and shout for me.

The allusions are not just to Achilles' wrath in the *Iliad* and his subsequent death but also to his reluctance for the battle. The final image is filtered through the tradition (mentioned in Greek literature) that Greek and Persian soldiers in the early fifth century BCE were comforted in their fear and spurred to greater efforts by the appearance of mythological heroes alongside them at the height of their danger. There is also a poetic allusion to Keats's claim that he was 'in the trenches' with Achilles. The transposition of Greek emblems and allusions into corresponding modern experience allows the poet to hint at his emotions of anxiety, fear and loneliness while dignifying them with the reference to Achilles. Shaw-Stewart was killed in France in 1917.

The icons of Troy, Helen and Achilles already had a special significance in providing critical and ironic foils for early twentieth-century poets. In an early poem, 'Menelaus and Helen' (1909), Rupert Brooke explored the contrast between poetic celebration of the Trojan war and the harsh unheroic 'realities' of its aftermath for the survivors:

> So far the poet. How should he behold
> That journey home, the long connubial years?
> ... So Menelaus nagged; and Helen cried;
> And Paris slept on by Scamander side.
> *The Poetical Works of Rupert Brooke,*
> ed. G. Keynes (1970)

Yeats used the Helen/Troy image in 'No Second Troy' to lay bare and in a sense to limit the effect of his former love (Maud Gonne) on himself and on the Irish nationalist uprising of 1916. Maud Gonne introduced Yeats to the Irish Republican Brotherhood. She married John MacBride, who was executed by the British in 1916.

> Why should I blame her that she filled my days
> With misery, or that she would of late
> Have taught to ignorant men most violent ways

The poem interweaves public and private aspects of the Helen/Menelaus/Paris triangle. The closing lines play on the Menelaus/Yeats correspondence of situation but then undercut the possibilities of a direct analogy:

... Why, what could she have done, being what she is?
Was there another Troy for her to burn?
'The Green Helmet and Other Poems' (1918),
Collected Poems (1968)

In 1916 Ezra Pound (not a combatant) invoked the historical force of the image of Troy directly through translation of an epigram of Agathias (*c.* 531 – *c.* 580 CE) –

Troy
Whither, O city, are your profits and your gilded shrine, ...
Time's tooth is into the lot, and war's and fate's too.
Envy has taken your all,
Save your douth [nobility] and your story.
The Oxford Book of Classical Verse in Translation,
no. 224, ed. Poole and Maule (1995)

As the war became more and more horrifying, Homeric images increasingly became emblems of the poetics of dilemma and compassion in the face of brutality and suffering. In 1916 Isaac Rosenberg's 'August 1914' alluded to the simile in *Iliad* 11.67-71:

And the men, like two lines of reapers who, facing each other,
drive their course all down the field of wheat or of barley
for a man blessed in substance, and the cut swathes drop
showering,
so Trojans and Achaians driving in against one another
cut men down, ...

trans. R.L. Lattimore

Rosenberg, who was killed in 1918, transfigured this simile into an image of the horror of mutual slaughter:

Iron are our lives
Molten right through our youth
A burnt space through ripe fields
A fair mouth's broken tooth
Rosenberg, *Collected Works* (1979)

3. The View from Translation: Image, Window and Dissection

In 'Break of Day in the Trenches' (1916) Rosenberg took another Homeric image and sardonically transplanted it away from its heroic associations:

> Poppies whose roots are in man's veins
> Drop, and are ever dropping;
> But mine in my ear is safe –
> Just a little white with the dust.

Homer's image of the poppy shaped a simile recording the death of one of Priam's sons, Gorgythion (*Iliad* 8.306-8):

> He bent drooping his head to one side, as a garden poppy
> bends beneath the weight of its yield and the rains of springtime;
> so his head bent slack to one side beneath the helm's weight.
>
> trans. R.L. Lattimore

Poppies were native to ancient Asia Minor, not just a phenomenon of First World War Flanders. The persistence of this poetic tradition is shown in the way the poppy has also been used as a referent by the Northern Irish poet Michael Longley (b. 1939), who incorporated a translation of Homer's simile into his own poem:

> *A Poppy*
> When millions march into the mincing machine
> An image in Homer picks out the individual
> Tommy and the doughboy in his doughboy helmet:
> 'Lolling to one side like a poppy in a garden
> Weighted down by its seed capsule and rainwater.
> His head drooped under the heavy, crestfallen
> Helmet' (an image Virgil steals – lasso papavera
> Collo – and so do I), and so Gorgythion dies,
> And the poppy that sheds its flower-heads in a day
> Grows in one summer four hundred more, which mean
> Two thousand petals overlapping as though to make
> A cape for a coin-goddess or a soldier's soul.
>
> Longley, *Broken Dishes* (1998)

Thus images from Homer can be a used to create layers of meaning, subverting public ideas about heroism, war and death by reinterpreting them in the light of personal experience. Homer was not the only classical poet who was refigured in this way. In his poem 'Dulce et decorum est', Wilfred Owen (1893-1918) followed the title with a series of images which challenge the notions that death in battle is a sign of individual heroism or justified by service to one's country:

> Bent double like old beggars under sacks,
> Knock-kneed, coughing like hags, we cursed
>   through sludge ...
> If in some smothering dreams you too could pace
> Behind the wagon that we flung him in,
> And watch the white eyes writhing in his face ...
> My friend, you would not tell with such high zest
> To children ardent for some desperate glory,
> The old Lie: Dulce et decorum est
> Pro patria mori.

Owen drafted the poem as a shell-shocked patient in Craiglockhart psychiatric hospital in Scotland in early October 1917. In a letter to his mother, he wrote: 'Here is a gas poem ... The famous Latin tag [from Horace, *Odes* III. ii.13] means of course "It is sweet and meet to die for one's country." Sweet! And decorous!'

The use by propagandists of this line from Horace in order to justify and console those who were likely to die and to glorify death in battle was another example of appropriation in the nineteenth and twentieth centuries of ideas and phrases from classical authors without much attention to the context in which they were originally written. Owen is in fact attacking not only the actual sentiments implied in such appropriation but also the ignorance, lack of imagination and sheer hypocrisy which underlay them. One could also compare, both poetically and morally Owen's reference to 'children ardent for some desperate glory' with Yeats's 'taught to ignorant men most violent ways'.

The persisting cultural force of Owen's devastating indictment of the Old Lie can be seen at the very end of the twentieth century in the song of the Martial Chorus in Derek Walcott's *The Odyssey: A Stage*

Version (performed by the Royal Shakespeare Company in 1992), in which Odysseus' encounter with the Cyclops takes place in a night-mare situation of political and military dictatorship in which the brain-washed troops keep the one-eyed tyrant in power. The Cyclops' Eye was represented by a periscope attachment, and Orwellian-style televisions in the early drafts of the script reinforced the allusions to surveillance and secret police. In this episode in Walcott's version the word-play in the bludgeon-like rhythm of the Martial Chorus uses the quotation from Horace and its associations with Owen as a bridge between the ironic exposure of the lies about 'good death' in battle and the implications for the psychological and intellectual survival of the individual.

> To die for the eye is best, it's the greatest glory
> Dulce et decorum est pro patria mori.
> There is no I after the eye, no more history ...
> > *The Odyssey: A Stage Version*,
> > act I, scene VII, p. 60

In addition to using classical referents as a startling literary device for demolishing easy assumptions, Owen also used Homer directly as the source of the poetic and structural force in his poem 'Strange Meeting' (drafted January-March 1918 in Yorkshire). The poem is also resonant with echoes from the Bible, Dante, Keats and Shelley, but two aspects are particularly important. First, there is the setting of the poem ('It seemed that out of battle I escaped') which involves a variation on the *katabasis* or descent to the Underworld which features in Homer, Vergil and Dante as a process of moral and spiritual enlightenment. Secondly, there are specific echoes of Homer's *Iliad* which in the concluding books explore the problematic relationships between the too easily polarised concepts of friends/enemies and courage/wisdom. Owen uses a variant of the epic device of *aristeia,* combat in which a hero demonstrates his courage, power and fighting skills, and gives it an unexpected turn at the end of the poem, when it emerges that it is the narrator himself who has been defeated and also that the issue of supremacy is no longer paramount. The concluding lines in the poem involve recognition 'I am the enemy you killed, my friend' and also resolution of enmity 'Let us sleep now'. The sequence picks up the words of Achilles in *Iliad* 21.106: 'So friend, you die also' (trans. R.L. Lattimore).

In *Iliad* book 24 the ultimate test of the resolution through suffering of the friend/enemy polarity occurs when the aged Priam goes to Achilles to plead for the return of the body of his son Hector, whom Achilles has killed, dishonouring his body and denying it burial. When the once mighty Priam becomes a supplicant he invokes the gods, Achilles' memory of his own father and Achilles' sense of pity:

> 'I have gone through what no other mortal on earth has gone
>   through;
> I put my lips to the hands of the man who has killed my children.'
> So he spoke and stirred in the other a passion of grieving
> for his own father. He took the old man's hand and pushed him
> gently away and the two remembered, as Priam sat huddled
> at the feet of Achilleus and wept close for manslaughtering Hector.
>   *Iliad* 24.505-10, trans. R.L. Lattimore

Michael Longley's poem on this theme is written in the context both of his extensive use of Homeric figures and images and of his exploration of the emotions generated by the Troubles in Northern Ireland in the last third of the twentieth century. He follows the Homeric order of events closely, except in one unique feature. Having described Achilles' response, his order that Hector's body be washed and prepared for Priam to carry it away, and the meal of mutual reconciliation, Longley *ends* with a translation of the action which brought about the recon- ciliation between the leaders of two warring communities:

> 'I get down on my knees and do what must be done
> And kiss Achilles' hand, the killer of my son.'
>   'Ceasefire', *The Ghost Orchid* (1995)

The title of Longley's poem alerts the reader to the fact that in Homer the episode was but an interlude in the long-running war which continued in the tradition outside the poem. Achilles and Priam, too, will die. The question of the permanence or otherwise of the modern equivalent of the truce is left open.

The effect of the final book of the *Iliad,* in its description of suffering and evocation of pity, is partly to counter-balance the parts of the poems which are primarily concerned with winning glory in battle. However, it also draws attention to the way in which even the most brutal parts of the poem explore the deepest aspects of human behaviour in the face of suffering and death. Similarly the most subtle and multi-layered 'war' poetry comes from those who move on from the more generalised or stereotypical mythological themes. These poets engage with the interrelationship between courage, aspiration, suffering, anger and grief which is found in Homer's poetry. They create some kind of equivalence. The transplantation and refiguration of Homer's poetics, that is of forms (including similes), direct speech, narrative which includes the feelings not only of the author but of other voices in the poem, the questioning of values, the communication of pathos, empathy, pity, rage and horror are found both in texts which sometimes specifically echo Homer and also in those which are more 'distant relatives'. Both kinds of engagement with Homeric themes and poetics are generated by the experiences and personal agonies of the writers and in most cases are expressed through poetic voices which empathise with or include the voices of others.

Some Homer critics have argued that the emotional depth and subtlety of *Iliad* 24 is uncharacteristic of the rest of the poem. Others claim that it is the culmination of its structural and poetic design. The debate is partly one about the genesis of the poem in oral culture and the whole question of authorship but it is also a debate about the balances of feelings, values and behaviours explored in the poem. Has a basically brutal narrative been refined by a skilful poet or poets? If so, does this confirm or challenge the view (of HD among others) that epic was masculine, harrowing and overbearingly hostile to finer feelings and moral awareness? I have argued that the writings of the war poets suggest that the various translational practices they developed to bring ancient and especially Homeric material into their work actually enhanced sensibility to the depth of human experience, enabling them to cross boundaries within their own culture as well as between ancient and modern.

The debate about the relationship between epic poetry and perceptions of war continues within the medium of translation itself. The 'Accounts' of Homer produced by the modern poet Christopher Logue (b. 1926) have not merely generated arguments between critics; they also involve interpretation of the main focus of the source epic. In this case the arguments about translation and interpretation are closely related. In contrast to some poetry and drama which draws on refigurations of Homer in Athenian tragedy as well as on epic and thus involves a double mediation of the Homeric tradition, Christopher Logue's work confronts Homeric epic directly. The publication process for Logue's versions of Homer is fragmented. Some of the work has appeared in small sections in journals and has only subsequently been published in a more integrated form. For example, *War Music* (1981) (described as 'An Account of Books 16 to 19 of Homer's *Iliad*) is divided into three sections, *Patrocleia*, *GBH* and *Pax*, of which only *GBH* had not been previously published. *Kings* ('An Account of Books One and Two of Homer's *Iliad*') was published in 1991 and *The Husbands* in 1994. This last is based on books 3 and 4 of the *Iliad*, plus some material from books 2, 5, 7 and 11. A section from *Iliad* 21 (Achilles at the Scamander) is included in *Selected Poems* (1996). This volume also features a translation of 'A Chorus from *Antigone*' ('There are many wonders on earth / and the greatest of these is man', Sophocles, *Antigone* 332f.), which includes these lines:

> Finding no enemy, we become our own enemy.
> As we trap the beasts, so we trap other men.
> But the others strike back, trap closing on trap.

The spareness of the language in this passage of translation and the interest in simile echo Logue's approach in his 'Accounts' of the *Iliad*. The 1996 collection also includes a number of poems which explore how experience challenges jingoistic or patriotic expectations of war, exposing the exploitative and the brutal, for example 'The Song of the Imperial Carrion', 'When I was Serving my Country' and 'The Song of the Dead Soldier':

> And then I saw a hag whose eyes
> Were big as medals, grey as lead ...
> The hag hissed warm, we met in blood,
> English shilling, Queen of Love.
> > *Selected Poems* (1996)

56

3. The View from Translation: Image, Window and Dissection

These poems help to locate the place of the Homeric 'Accounts' of Logue (who himself served in the Black Watch) in relation to his other work.

Another significant aspect of the production history of Logue's Homeric work is that much of it was written to be performed rather than to be read. The initial passages of the *Patrocleia* were created for BBC radio. *Kings* has been particularly successful in this respect, having been broadcast in full on BBC Radio 3 and performed in the theatre by Alan Howard at the National Theatre (September 1992) with Logue on stage. It has also been presented as performance poetry by Peter Florence at the Ledbury Poetry Festival in 1999 when a capacity audience sat transfixed. In interviews Logue has related this emphasis to his broader view of poetry, 'Poetry is not a silent art'. The 'Accounts', and especially *Kings,* are also shaped by Logue's interest in modern technology's ways of capturing the epic moment. In this respect cinematic approaches take on the role of a translational technique. Logue's concept of the 'moment' is also closely related to the moment of 'luminous detail' identified by Pound and to HD's metaphor of the window or portal, which served as a means of viewing and capturing a distinctive aspect of the source text.

Logue has commented in some detail on his approach to translation, initially in his introduction to *War Music* in which he states that since he had no knowledge of Greek, he began his work on the *Iliad* by studying translations by Chapman (1611), Pope (1720), Lord Derby (1865), A.T. Murray (1924) and Rieu (1950). He noted that 'while Pope was the most and Murray the least accomplished of these authors, Murray, according to learned gossip, possessed the most and Pope the least information about Homer's Greek' (ibid., p. vii). He also commented that each of the translations which he read gave a different impression of Homer. Logue therefore decided to keep to the outline of the story in the passages he had been asked to translate but to vary incidents and similes and on the whole to omit Homer's formulaic epithets – what Logue calls the 'thick-as-a-pyramid-Ajax' descriptions of the main figures, repeated at intervals throughout the poem. Subsequently Logue used literal translations which gave a better sense of Greek word order. He tried to make the voices of the characters 'come alive and to keep the action on the move'. His aim always was to produce a poem. The poem was to be 'dependent upon whatever, through reading and through conversation, I could guess about a small part of the *Iliad*' (ibid., p. viii).

The project thus combined the intention to create a poem in English with Logue's analysis of the naked spine in Homer which joined episodes of the *Iliad*. The *Patrocleia* (book 16) he thought contained the 'cruel twist' that the death of Patroclus ensured the destruction of Troy by motivating Achilles to return to the battle. *Pax* (book 19) involved the resolution of conflict between the allies through material compensation, sanctioned by formal sacrifice. The two episodes were bridged by *GBH* (or Grievous Bodily Harm, described by Logue as 'an English legal term for serious forms of criminal assault': books 17 and 18). This consisted of just over 600 lines devoted to mass violence. Significantly, Logue also refers to the critical support received from what he describes as 'the hard core of Unprofessional Ancient Greek Readers, Homer's lay fans'. He has written of the translations of Knox, Fagles and Lattimore: 'these three professors have been reading Homer all their lives but he's failed to teach them what verse is. They do not write verse. They write blank-verse prose.'[4] There is in Logue's interviews and prose writing a sometimes explicit opposition between his desire to create an English poem which communicates dominant features of Homer and the response of academic critics, hostile both to his means of doing so and to his identification of those features.

In *War Music*, Logue developed a narrative technique ('Now hear this') which accelerated into the account of the fighting carrying the reader/listener with occasional prods such as 'Imagine wolves' (p. 12), 'you will have heard about the restless mice' (p. 17), and 'See if you can imagine how it looked' (p. 19). The language and rhythm are direct and unadorned:

> Picture a yacht
> Cantering at speed
> Over ripple-ribbed sand
> Change its mast to a man
> Change its boom to a bow
> Change its sail to a shield
> See Menelaos.
> *GBH*, *War Music*, p. 38 (1981)

3. The View from Translation: Image, Window and Dissection

Even the typography expresses the visual dynamics, with intersections of large print and a double-page spread to convey the impact when APOLLO struck (p. 30). The compression of description and speech serve to amplify the effect of the violence. The omissions are significant – the description of Achilles' shield; Briseis' lamentation of Patroclus; the intervention of Athena. Anachronism is flaunted; the yacht quoted above and cars, vampires, planes, Cape Kennedy are only a small selection.

In the Introduction to *Kings* Logue repeats his intentions about live voices, dynamic action and the creation of a poem in English which is both autonomous in style and dependent on Homer. In this work the film technique of visual 'windows' is explicit, with the directions included as voices in the text: 'Reverse the shot. Go close. Hear Agamemnon' (p. 16). This signposting is in contrast to Homer where the inter-related levels of the audience's 'knowledge' of what is to happen are assumed as part of the audience's frame of reference. Logue's technique, like film, directs the gaze, but unlike film his poems acknowledge this openly. In the same way Logue's adaptation of the technique of the epic simile (and especially of the way in which it draws the audience's experience into the poem and frames interpretation in the context of the receiving audience's culture) is explicit. Logue's diction demythologises – 'Cuntstruck Agamemnon' (p. 19) – and even the figurative language reduces heroes to the lowest forms of nature, 'fearful as the toad in a python's mouth' (p. 7). The ruthless and unquestioned exploitation of women and the rank and file is never concealed (p. 5; cf. *Iliad* 23.705, where a woman is valued at four oxen):

> And 30 fertile women
> As is required …
> Were sorted by the herald's staff and then
> Soon after sunrise on the following day
> Led to the common sand for distribution.

The idea of reciprocity, so complex and sensitively shaded in Owen's and Longley's responses to Homer, is reduced to basic material exchange. To expose the brutal basis for the conduct of war Logue strips Homer's poetry of debate, empathy and compassion and devastatingly reveals material greed, psychological and physical brutality and the ruthless exercise of power. In Homer pathos and compassion derive their power from the contrast with the raw violence of the very situation within which the finer qualities are displayed. Logue's poetics construct a window in the crude sub-surface of the Homeric text. That this unadorned and unmitigated power speaks across the centuries is deeply discomforting. The harsh masculine competitive ethos which ascribes no identity or humanity to women or ordinary people reminds us of the 'unacceptable face' of the culture represented in Homer, but in Homer these are mitigated by the emotional and moral sensitivity of the poetry of books 6 (Hector and Andromache at Troy), 9 (the debate about the relationship between privilege and military obligation) and 24 (the retrieval of Hector's body and his funeral). Disturbingly, *War Music, Kings,* and *Husbands* cover the various aspects of public and private power relationships, which are subsumed under the Homeric words for leader, ruler and master, *anax* and *basileus*. Logue's dissection brings the reader/listener face to face with the question whether and how the poetic force of the treatment of heroic rivalry and death in Homer functions, then and subsequently, as a justification and a sanction of the underlying social values exposed by Logue. The almost unspeakable question then becomes, was Homeric epic complicit in perpetrating the great Lie?

Critical reaction to Logue's 'Accounts' has sometimes been incandescent. Even George Steiner, who regards Logue as a significant figure (almost of genius) in Homer translation, describes him as 'feeding on the original for his own increase' (*After Babel*, 423) and therefore *over*crowding, heightening and dramatising the text, while Professor Bernard Knox in a review article has described Logue's approach to translation as trivialising and vulgar sensationalism. The two examples of criticism point to different features. Steiner's points to the power of Logue's writing and its rhetorical *effect,* in spite or because of the spareness of much of the writing. Knox points to the violence and cruelty which are emphasised in Logue's interpretation of Homer and to the means which Logue uses both to capture this and to communicate it through the language and aesthetic categories of modern 'popular' art forms. If the high moral seriousness of Homer is accepted as a coherent and structured aspect of the poem as a whole, then to subvert this aesthetically and ideologically can be seen as bordering on sacrilege. The desanitisation of Homer by Logue is a revolutionary intervention (on a far deeper level than that of mere protest poetry) both aesthetically and ideologically. Critical reaction to Logue's work raises significant general questions about the relationship between criticism of the aesthetics of a translation and criticism of its revisionist or interventionist role in challenging traditional norms of interpretation as well as of translation. These debates show that it is not only translational norms but also the classical tradition itself which is fiercely contested.

4

Translation as Critique
and Intervention

Truth is an arrow, poisoned to all hasty archers!
Even bending the bow is much. The arrow will still be an
Arrow if found among rushes. Truth dressed as a lie is still truth
And the bow won't die with the archer.

Heiner Müller, 'Tales of Homer' (1975)

This chapter considers the role of translation in challenging political and cultural orthodoxy. Müller's poem 'Tales of Homer' takes as its inspiration the passage in *Iliad* 2.216-77 in which Thersites ('the ugliest man who came beneath Ilion', in Lattimore's version) challenges the way Agamemnon has exploited the Greek fighters in order to gain plunder for himself. Thersites is then himself attacked and ridiculed. Müller imagines Homer as a kind of Socrates responding to questions from his pupils. When asked why he has put the truth about the war into the mouth of Thersites and thus allowed it to be discredited, the poet replies that he wanted to be 'liked by princes', to avoid hunger and, perhaps, to gain fame. This implied claim that the epic poet depends on the realities of the power structure is one response to the questions put by the pupils, but in the next stanza Müller makes Homer elaborate. Truth is dangerous (as much to the archer/poet as to the recipient of the arrow) because, even when masked and discredited, as in the Thersites episode, the arrow of truth retains its powers of survival and its potential to be retrieved and used by others apart from the original archer.

Müller (1929-95) wrote his major works in Soviet-dominated East Germany, called the German Democratic Republic after the post-Second World War partition of Germany. His early work was concerned with the social and economic difficulties of the GDR, but political

63

censorship made it difficult for him to have his plays performed, and in the 1960s he turned to Greek and Roman subject matter, partly in order to create a political and social distance between his writing and the perceptions of the censors. He translated Sophocles' *Oedipus Tyrannus* (1965) and the *Prometheus Bound* attributed to Aeschylus (1967-8). These were preceded by *Philoktet* (1958-64), based on Sophocles' *Philoctetes,* and *Herakles 5*, a farcical variation on the satyr play, dramatising the cleansing of the Augean stables.

Müller's political aim in reworking classical material is proclaimed in his close translation into German of Horace *Satire* II.I.[1] In this poem Horace discusses with his legal adviser Trebatius the dangers of writing poetry which is both public and critical of the powerful, who will retaliate viciously. The translation ends abruptly with the lines:

> Nich allzeit
> Hat Cäser für Horaz ein offnes Ohr.
> Wird er verkehrt gestreichelt, schlägt er aus.

(Caesar does not always listen receptively to Horace. If he is rubbed up the wrong way, he lashes out.)

It has frequently been pointed out that many of the major post-war East German writers were stimulated by classical texts and adapted and reworked them to circumvent suppression of their work.[2] The reasons for this are, however, not as simple as they may at first seem. To translate and rework classical sources was not simply to invoke some sort of secret code which anyway could be 'read' only by those with detailed knowledge of the source text. To be effective, reworking of the ancient material had both to be permitted by the authorities *and* to communicate to readers and audiences. In identifying the main features of the underlying cultural context which stimulated this phenomenon in the GDR it is necessary also to point to factors which have parallels in other post-war socio-political contexts. In the rest of this chapter and in the next, this will lead to the discussion of further examples of ways in which 'the archer's arrows' have found political and cultural targets through translation and adaptation of classical material. It will also illuminate aspects of the relationship between writers and societies which are under pressure or feel threatened by change.

4. Translation as Critique and Intervention

In the GDR there was a further paradox in that, while classical education had been cut back in both schools and universities, probably for economic reasons, Marxist theory and practice also recognised that the revolutionary proletariat could assimilate and refashion what was of value in pre-revolutionary human thought and culture.[3] This idea was developed into an officially sanctioned concept called Kulturelles Erbe or Erworbene Tradition which involved preserving what Walter Ulbricht, President of the GDR, called 'the great tradition of our humanistic heritage'. However, this was prevented from becoming a simplistic propagandist appropriation by the fact that German cultural tradition already had models for the critical use of classical referents (Flashar, 1991). In the twentieth century the shaping force in this respect was Bertold Brecht, whose work demonstrated that variations on classical sources could be ideologically acceptable to socialists as a basis for political statements and explorations. Brecht also sharpened the potential of classical texts and images to form the basis of critique, which in his case was directed mainly against fascism and capitalism. He used a variety of dramatic and poetic techniques which both emphasised the distance and difference between ancient and modern yet also pointed to parallels and resonances which prompted readers and audiences to think analytically and critically about the modern as well as the ancient images and figures.

A Brechtian prototype, playing with the form of the epic simile, juxtaposed Hitler, after the Reichstag fire of 1934, with the Emperor Nero:

> The Roman emperor Nero, who
> also wanted to pass for a great artist, is said
> to have played the harp on a tower
> looking down on Rome as it burned at his command.
> On a similar occasion
> the Führer watching a high house burn
> took out his pencil and briskly drew a
> plan for a splendid new building. So – in the manner of
>   their art –
> the two differed.
>   *Werkausgabe Suhrkamp* IX 525 (1967)[4]

Exiled during the fascist regime in Germany, Brecht returned from the USA in 1947. In 1948 his version of Sophocles' *Antigone* took poetic allusion into the theatre, equating Creon with Hitler as an embodiment of fascist dictatorship. Brecht's *Antigone* was widely interpreted as showing how the principled individual could resist totalitarianism. The design (by Casper Neher) was formal and minimalist, including nothing which would intervene between the audience's awareness and the impact of the actors telling the story. The actors, in plain black robes, remained on the stage throughout, seated in a semi-circle at the rear. The playing space was delineated by four tall poles topped with horse skulls, and a rack of masks was used to represent the Theban elders.[5] In the staging Creon was played as equivalent to Hitler, but of course the theme of resistance to tyranny could be interpreted as referring to other kinds of régime.

Brecht also used his analysis of classical literature and history as a basis for identifying silences which masked the marginalised or completely absent voices of the oppressed. The seminal example is his poem 'Fragen eines lesenden Arbeiters' ('Questions from a worker who reads'):

> Wer baute das siebentorige Theben?
> In der Büchern stehen die Namen von Königen.
> Haben die Könige die Felsbrocken herbei geschleppt?

> Who built Thebes of the seven gates?
> In the books you will find the names of kings.
> Did the kings haul up the lumps of rock?

Brecht, *Poems*, trans. N. Replansky (1979)[6]

Brecht's return to Europe symbolised the revival of the left-wing politically committed theatre of the 1920s and 1930s which had been crushed by Fascism. The aesthetic of the socialist theatre had been formulated by practitioners such as Erwin Piscator (1893-1968) as well as Brecht. It re-emerged after the Second World War, influencing politically engaged theatre world-wide, up to and including the late twentieth-century adaptations of Greek drama and poetry discussed in later chapters.

4. Translation as Critique and Intervention

Piscator inaugurated the notion of 'engaged' theatre among the avant-garde in Germany during the 1920s with a committed self-styled 'proletarian' theatre practice. This aimed to alter the consciousness of the spectator by developing an anti-naturalist aesthetic, using topical, historical and factual material such as newspaper reports and photographs. The 'message' could be spoken or sung by a chorus, on stage or in the auditorium. In some cases the (then) new technology of film could be used to create a visual 'montage' effect of narrative interrupted by or simultaneous with the action. This approach has become known as the theatre of *intervention*. Intervention was a vital shaping force in critique. It aimed to create an awareness of the underlying ideology supporting the continuation of the status quo and/or the subjection of the situation to critique.

Piscator and Brecht differed in their views on how this could best be achieved.[7] Piscator believed in moving the audience and thought that in so doing 'epic' required largeness of scale and narrative. Brecht thought that coolness, detachment and stimulation of thought were required, hence the Verfremdungseffekt (distancing or alienation) created in his staging of the *Antigone*. Both, however, shared the view that theatre was a weapon to be used in struggle and that the value and extent of intervention depended on the immediate theatrical and cultural context.

The practice of Intervention as critique can therefore operate on two levels. First, it can involve a theatre of opposition, protest or resistance, taking the place of open political dissent when opposition movements are banned and dispersed or censorship most severe (for example, during the apartheid regime in South Africa). In this context it also gives 'outsiders' an alternative view of what is happening in a society. Secondly, the practice and techniques of Intervention can be effective as cultural critique in helping readers and audiences to identify and debate underlying ideologies and social structures (which may be glossed over even in apparently more liberal societies or in those undergoing rapid change). It is this aspect which will be examined in the chapters that follow. In both categories of Intervention, the role of classical sources and referents may be crucial, either as a means of 'distancing' debate about current issues by using a remote mythological setting or as a means of inducing cultural shock by suggesting more overt correspondences and equivalences between ancient and modern crises and debates in a way which destabilises modern certainties. In both categories, a transformation of audience perspectives is a prime goal.

The dual effect of the Marxist acceptance of the cultural value of classical source texts in terms both of their role in human history and of their potential for reinterpretation and reworking, together with the example of Brecht's deployment of classical referents as the basis for critique, underlies a web of formal, discursive and contextual elements in the translation and adaptation of classical texts. Brecht's theory of 'alienation' could be invoked to support the use of texts and figures from the remote past. The remoteness in both time and culture created a critical distance, which enabled a detached analysis of how the artistic work of the past was being re-interpreted in a modern situation. The ancient material provided a foil against which modern applications could be created and communicated. The whole process demonstrates that while the classical material provided a simple stability of reference, its significance was not irrevocably bound ideologically to any one system but could be redefined to open up new associations and thus play a role in transforming perceptions and understanding of both ancient and modern situations and metaphors.

Furthermore, these new perceptions and relationships might be fluid rather than monolithic or didactic. Both Greek and Roman source material was framed by the artists' sometimes uneasy relationship with patronage (whether in the competitive context of the Greek dramatic festivals or the situation of the Roman poet in relation to the authority of the patron or the Emperor). The modern artist, too, could for political reasons mask critique with literary and dramatic guile. This 'masking' is analogous to the way rushes conceal the arrows in Müller's poem 'Tales of Homer'. The original bowman (Homer, Sophocles, Horace) might no longer be active (because of the passage of time and the marginalisation of ancient culture) but the arrow could be recovered and redirected by a new archer. The redirection takes place through the medium of different aspects of translation and its associated techniques. These are shaped partly by the underlying cultural traditions in the receiving society, including assumptions both in the dominant groups and in the target audience about the ideology and values of classical texts. They are also shaped by the aims of the authors in seeking to transform perspectives on the relationship be-

68

tween ancient and modern and therefore on the way in which modern situations and processes are perceived. A further shaping force is derived from the formal elements in the source texts, the adaptability of these elements and the potential for the ancient poetic images and metaphors to resonate in a new cultural context. All these aspects come together in the new work, whether translation or adaptation, to produce an enactment of equivalence between ancient and modern material. This equivalence may tend towards the closed, for example using an ancient narrative as an allegory of a modern situation, or remain open, playing on difference as well as correspondences, deferring certainties and thus avoiding ideological rejection. Therefore the image of the 'truth' carried by the arrow needs to be equated with notions of sharpness of insight rather than with specific dogma.

Müller's classical work is characterised by precisely this kind of deferral of certainty or even of interpretation. Because his early realistic drama about land reform had led to his expulsion from the East German Writers' Union in 1961 and to the banning of the production and publication of his work, it was too easy for western writers and critics who 'discovered' his work in the 1970s to assume that it was motivated entirely by antipathy to the Stalinist régime in East Germany. Such illusions were in any case to be rudely shattered when in 1993 it was revealed that, at least since the 1970s, Müller had had discussions with the Stasi (secret police) about fellow artists. In a series of often contradictory interviews, Müller asserted that the conversations were simply about cultural politics and claimed a lack of interest in political and moral matters, saying that he regarded great events, socialism and his own relationships as 'drama' in themselves. For this reason, he said, he did not speak out on behalf of dissidents and regarded ideas as 'material' to be played with, while art was 'a space of irresponsibility ... [and] freedom'.

The problematic discovery of 'truth' in an uncongenial context which he envisaged in his Homer poem was enacted in his adaptation of Sophocles' *Philoctetes*. Müller's *Philoktet* was initially thought to be modelled on the theatrical power of a Brechtian Lehrstück, a play in which the actors themselves participated in order to undergo a personal transformation, a learning experience. The concept required a style which was for the benefit of the actors, not the spectators. The role of the Chorus was important in a Lehrstück since it provided a collective voice or judgement with which the individual had to engage. However, most realisations of Müller's *Philoktet* have been by professional actors who have not regarded roles in the play as a means to bring about performative change in their own outlook. In Sophocles' play the main figure, suffering from a noxious snake bite and literally isolated from his own comrades, the Greeks, is to be tricked into giving up his infallible weapon, the bow of Heracles, so that it can be used to ensure the victory of the Greeks at Troy, but is eventually persuaded to rejoin the expedition voluntarily. Müller's adaptation, initially regarded as an allegory applying the Greek myth to Stalinism, in fact makes profound changes from the Sophoclean treatment.

Müller's use of other writers (whether Sophocles, Brecht or Shakespeare) was sometimes criticised as mere plagiarism and mimicry. Certainly, he followed Brecht in regarding texts by others as stimuli to refiguration rather than as inviolable private property and his imagery concerning the process is predatory – 'to know [the dead] you have to eat them and then you spit out the living particles'.[8] He also related this obsession with ancient texts to modernity – 'Necrophilia is love of the future. One has to accept the presence of the dead as dialogue partners or dialogue disturbers – the future will emerge only out of dialogue with the dead.'[9] In the coup de théâtre at the close of Müller's *Philoktet*, Neoptolemus, functioning as Odysseus' apprentice, actually kills Philoctetes. Müller's change prevents easy interpretations. In this reversal of Sophocles' closure, it may be that it is Odysseus who represents right ordering and the primacy of the needs of the state; although the state is hard and unforgiving, its work has to be done and Odysseus is authentic, if unheroic (Philoctetes and Neoptolemus, too, are deheroised). The emblem of private honour, represented in the return of the bow, is discredited. Equally, there is no unflawed socialist ideological victory. The truth, to which Müller referred in his Homer poem, may be represented in an unpalatable context. Odysseus is unpleasantly honest; cheating is called cheating, a massacre is referred to as a massacre, a lie as a lie (but nevertheless to be borne). Odysseus and Neoptolemus are to tell the Greeks that Philoctetes was a hero killed by Trojans, but it is actually Neoptolemus' action which has 'ended both his injury and ours'.[10]

Müller's *Philoktet* was first performed in Munich in 1968, directed by Hans Lutzan who subsequently staged the play in Hamburg, West

Berlin and Venice. In the GDR the play was performed in Leipzig by students (1974) but not professionally premiered until 1977, in East Berlin. It was also staged in Poland in 1976. It is widely accepted as difficult to interpret. Even autocratic direction cannot unequivocally focus the audience response. Müller used the term 'veiling' (Verschleierung) to describe the definitive and manipulative directorial choices which can limit interpretative possibilities in performance. Partly for this reason he went on to experiment with collage constructions that disrupted realistic narrative with mythical interludes (for example in *Zement*, 1972). He dispensed entirely with narratives and moved to pastiches, thematically linked with dense webs of quotation from German history and myth. Eventually he adapted this approach to create the *Medeamaterial* (full title: *Verkommenes Ufer Medeamaterial Landschaft mit Argonauten* [*Despoiled Shore Medea Material Landscape with Argonauts*]), premiered in 1983 in Bochum. This sealed his move away from verbal tautness and into cross-genre experiment. These stages in Müller's refiguring of classical narratives and motifs map his development as an artist and demonstrate the aesthetic and political slipperiness of his works.

Müller's development of the concept of *Material* was part of a strategy to prevent uniform interpretation. The aim was to produce an artistic work which could be tilted in different directions to enable different perspectives to emerge. This kind of text was, he thought, 'productive' in that productive texts could activate those who came in contact with them. The spectator was supposed to be an active 'translator', not a passive consumer, and this could be supported by direction and by acting styles. For instance, actors could adopt a neutral style of delivery in order to defer interpretation and put the onus on the spectator. Directors could also support the 'productivity' of the work by ensuring that staging generated a variety of possible interpretations and thus did not restrict the spectators' engagement with the play.

In the context of the organisation and structures of German theatre, and especially those of the GDR, this was a subversive approach. Theatre was heavily subsidised, which one might have thought would encourage innovation by limiting the role of commercial pressures. However, each theatre was under the management of an Intendant who had the power to shape and control artistic output, especially by choice of Dramaturg and Director. In German theatre the Dramaturg has traditionally been responsible for researching the implications of the text for choice of costumes, stage properties and contextual and intertextual aspects of production (including adaptation or abridgement of the text). The Dramaturg might form a productive relationship with the Director, who traditionally tended also to build up an ensemble of relatively low profile actors.[11] Statistical analysis of the numbers of productions of Müller's plays in the GDR as a proportion of the total numbers of stagings of all plays shows that they received serious attention only in the final years of the GDR (1987-9), whereas in other German-speaking countries (Federal Republic of Germany, Austria, Switzerland) there was evidence of sustained interest throughout the 1980s. In the 1990s, by contrast, once the Berlin Wall was dismantled and Germany reunited, performance of Müller's plays seemed to have lost its public raison d'être as a theatrical expression of political dissent or uncertainty, although it is possible that his death in 1995 stimulated interest in the broader relationship between aesthetic diversity and socio-political debate. His work has also been influential in America, particularly in the stagings of European drama developed by Robert Wilson. Wilson explored the themes of death and renewal in Greek mythology, drawing on Müller's conception of displacement of interpretation.

Medeamaterial is the best documented of Müller's montage works. The three sections were devised and created over a period spanning 1949-82 with various revisions (published text in *Herzstück*, *Texte 7*, Berlin, Rotbuch, 1983). The parts of the triptych are very different. The first, 'Despoiled Shore', is a phantasm of impressions (attributed in the early editions to a chorus); from these emerges the face of Medea. The second part, 'Medea Material', is a dramatic dialogue (of which the centrepiece is a speech by Medea). The third, 'Landscape with Argonauts', is a first-person monologue ranging over a modern landscape of consumerism and alienation.

The world premiere of the work took place on 22 April 1983 in the Schauspielhaus Bochum, with which Müller was closely associated. The production was directed by Manfred Karge and Matthias Langhoff, who played the role of Jason. Kirsten Dene was Medea. The spectators were offered two kinds of introductory guidance. In the foyer of the theatre was an exhibition illustrating sections of the text – for example, a pack of condoms, a map of Germany with a lake to the

4. Translation as Critique and Intervention

East of Berlin coloured in red, a broken-off chair leg. A critic called this an Argonaut museum. Secondly, the 492-page programme included a lexicon of references and texts of several of Müller's classical adaptations and of Apollonius Rhodius' *Argonautica* (a Greek epic of the third century BCE).

In the theatre itself there was no integrated theatrical language of visual and verbal signs to help the audience translate the meaning of Euripides' or Müller's work. The set was the same for all three parts. Wreckage of the Argo was suspended over the heads of the audience, while the stage was littered with unlabelled tin cans and dominated by an aircraft propeller. In the midst of these tokens of modern technology, domesticity was represented by chairs for the cast and a basin plumbed into the wall (for a detailed account see Barnett, pp. 229-32). Jason wore a bald latex mask which covered his head and made facial expression impossible. Medea's 'mask' used make-up to accentuate her age and loss of looks. In the first sequence of the 'Medea Material' Medea mimed vomiting into the basin and then looked at herself in the mirror with a howl of recognition, 'This is not Medea'. Her monologue was divided into blocks punctuated by gaps filled with howls and shrieks; her sons were represented by two cans of corned beef, the contents squashed in her hands. In contrast, Jason was measured and restrained, responding to Medea's words only at the point when he symbolically strangled and raped her. In the third part ('Landscape with Argonauts') the Nurse and Medea remained dead on stage, Medea strangled with her pearls, tongue protruding. Jason, jogging on the spot, recited in an emotionally neutral style, with projected footage of an aircraft's circular manoeuvres.

There seemed, indeed, to be no single system of reference into which Medea could be integrated, no defined framework of translation. As with Müller's *Philoktet*, the death of the supposed protagonist prevented coherent correspondences between ancient and modern. Further productions in Germany (Stuttgart 1983, Munich 1984) tried to convey a greater integration between the three parts of the montage. Even so, critics were frustrated by the contrast between the associative and allegorical possibilities of the text and the deliberately limiting context set by the staging and acting styles. Later productions in Berlin (1987) experimented with an older actress who, situated in a rundown recording studio, could appear to be looking back, and in the first sequence set a tone of irreverence as, dressed in an army greatcoat with a clown's nose, she pushed over a life-size effigy of Müller.

By contrast, in Düsseldorf in 1989 the audience was divided according to gender and seated opposite one another with the playing area in the middle. Thus each gender could watch both the two actors and the reactions of the other gender. The actors were described in the programme as 'Frau' (Woman) and 'Mann' (Man). They acted as chorus leaders, encouraging their respective gender blocks to join in and chant the lines against each other. The audience was encouraged to dance with the actors in the playing space, almost becoming participants as in a Lehrstück. Throughout, music and simple stage properties (such as a Polaroid camera) emphasised associative aspects of the spoken text. The effect was to emphasise gender conflict rather than to suggest diverse socio-critical or historical readings as in the other productions. These different ways of staging the montage with very similar spoken text illustrate how the 'material' technique can make both character and plot problematic and, in confronting the audience with open and opaque experiences, move away from and challenge referential or thematic aspects of translation technique. That this work has been so diversely staged demonstrates how the processes of translation can be progressively displaced from the author through the staging and the experience of the audience. In Müller's work Philoctetes' arrow delivers no unproblematic truth, but rather a rebarbative displacement of certainty.

However, the main transformative elements identified here – intervention, the manipulation of critical distance, the impact on the actors and audience of a Lehrstück experience and aesthetic transposition – can interact in a very different way in different cultural and political contexts. Examples of the creation and reception of translations of Greek material in South Africa suggest that a sense of aesthetic shock may be an initial symptom of cultural, political and ideological rejection of the interventionist impact of modern productions of Greek drama. A study by Professor Piet Conradie of theatrical reviews and critical comments on twentieth-century performances of Greek plays translated into English or Afrikaans in South Africa shows that initial surprise that translations of Greek plays could move modern audiences gives way to awareness of how the emotional impact of the play was shaped and directed by performance style and staging. In April 1944 a production of Euripides' *Trojan Women* in Stellenbosch and Cape Town by Die Kunsskool van Kaapstad marked the first staging of an Afrikaans prose translation (by J.P.J. van Rensburg, a university professor). A reviewer commented: 'It is true of all times that women and children suffer the most during a war, but also that the conquerors are bringers of calamity and misfortune.'[12] The poet N.P. van Wyk Louw was also astonished: 'The emotional impact of such a play is really incredible. I have sat listening to it five times in all with tears in my eyes ... simplicity indeed, but also obscurity, savageness, virtually unrestrained emotionality ... many who have seen the play produced in Europe, claimed that this time it was more beautiful, specially [*sic*] more human; no stylised, static acting as if the Greeks were Greek Statues ... the chorus became real people, not merely "a static row of musical instruments" ' (trans. Conradie). In 1944 Euripides' play spoke with particular clarity to a war-weary world in which the difference in degree of suffering between victors and vanquished had become increasingly blurred.

Nevertheless, the resonances of Greek drama from a particular time and a particular play can be threatening as well as cathartic. This became evident in the debate about the 1981 Cape Performing Arts Board production of Aeschylus, *Oresteia*, directed by Dieter Reible in an Afrikaans version by Merwe Scholtz of Walter Jens' adaptation. This was intended as a prestige production, but Reible's production style was regarded as controversial, and attempts to stress the cultural value of the production backfired. Scholtz wrote 'In the *Oresteia* extremely important moral and juridical values are thought through completely for the first time in our history ... nothing, surely, can be wrong with a trilogy which shows how man progresses from the primitive conception of the blood-feud to an idealistic view of a harmonious and just society' (trans. Conradie). Audiences, however, were more attuned to a traditionally stylised 'classical' style of production which distanced them from the emotional implications of the play, and they reacted against the neon lights, smoke, gory corpses on trolleys and chanting which seemed far from the 'measure and proportion' (to quote one newspaper letter-writer) that they expected of Greek drama. In the 1980s the apartheid regime in South Africa was still in place if increasingly beleaguered, and contemporary resonances might be re-

sisted by conservative white audiences. Another theatrical flop oc-
curred in 1985 when a Cape Performing Arts Board production of
Sophocles' *Antigone* had to close prematurely. Apparently leaflets pro-
claiming 'Free Antigone', distributed to encourage people to attend,
had been assumed to be subversive propaganda.

However, in a directly interventionist context the *Antigone* could
indeed speak to the condition of South Africa. In the 1960s the Serpent
Players, a group of black actors based in New Brighton (a township
outside Port Elizabeth) and closely associated with the actor, poet and
playwright Athol Fugard, had included Greek tragedies in its reper-
toire. In July 1965 they prepared to stage Sophocles' *Antigone*, but just
before the opening performance one of the leading actors, Norman
Ntshinga, was imprisoned on Robben Island for alleged political of-
fences. There he arranged a performance of the play by prisoners.
These events inspired *The Island*, a collaboration between Fugard,
Winston Ntshona and John Kani, which was first performed in 1973
at the Space Theatre in Cape Town. The play depicts the suffering of
political prisoners on Robben Island and the climax is their performance, in a play within a play, of a version of the *agon* or confrontation
between Antigone and Creon in Sophocles' *Antigone*. *The Island* was
subsequently presented worldwide and became an icon for its denun-
ciation of the brutality and injustice of the apartheid regime.[13] There
is eloquent testimony to the impact of the Robben Island improvisation
as itself a Lehrstück from the first President of a free South Africa,
Nelson Mandela. He recorded in his memoirs his own participation in
the *Antigone* while a prisoner on Robben Island and commented on
Antigone's significance for his own struggle: 'She was in her own way
a freedom fighter, for she defied the law on the ground that it was
unjust.' Equally, however, his own playing of the role of Creon enabled
him to confront, in prospect, the responsibilities of power: '[Creon's]
inflexibility and blindness ill become a leader, for a leader must temper
justice with mercy.'[14]

Since the end of apartheid, Greek drama has continued to develop
its role in intervention, and this has involved the creation of new work
drawing on both Greek and African culture. Productions have focussed
on the correspondences between ancient myths and contemporary
situations and between Greek and African myth. There has also been
a fruitful interaction between different art forms, especially drama

and dance. A notable example is the adaptation of Euripides' *Medea*, directed by Mark Fleishman and Jennie Reznek, which has been performed in Cape Town, Grahamstown and Johannesburg (October 1994 – March 1996). As well as drawing on Euripides, the adaptation was influenced by Seneca's version of the myth. It also included material from Apollonius of Rhodes' epic *Argonautica* and some ideas from Müller's *Medeamaterial*. The production involved a creative collaboration between the directors and a multi-racial cast of actors and dancers, the latter from the Jazzart Dance Theatre. Jazzart had developed as a collective cultural project aiming to construct an alternative ideology to apartheid. Its special contribution was to promote understanding and valuing of cultural diversity and exchange and to enact alternative forms of empowerment. The text of the play was created through study of different versions of the Medea myth, improvisation and workshop experiment. Mime and dance were used to suggest meaning through the body language of the cast and the spoken script was multilingual, including Xhosa, Tamil and Afrikaans as well as the English of the main part of the text. English was spoken without an Afrikaner accent.[15]

The overall aim of the *Medea* adaptation was both to offer aspects of Lehrstück experience to the cast (who were able to respond personally to the material in a way that reflected their own experiences) and to create an interventionist theatrical experience for the audience, who were encouraged to relate the marginalised and 'barbarian' Medea to those excluded and tyrannised by apartheid and to view Jason as a man who held that violation of human rights was acceptable as a means to power. The Senecan version of the myth was followed, in which Medea was ordered to leave her children behind and go into exile alone. This was thought to make Medea's plight even more sympathetic to the audience. There was no strong religious ambience, but Medea's magical powers were made prominent.

Critical response to the production was varied, although most acknowledged that the staging transformed classical material in the light of current issues. One claimed that 'it holds a mirror up to the gratuitous violence, brutality and racial xenophobia of South Africa today' (M. Jenkins, 'A Medea for Today', *The Citizen*, 1 February 1996, 23). Another perceived and rejected a process of 'Africanisation' in the staging (A. Bristowe, 'Beating the Wrong Drum', *The Star*, 1 February

1996). It is thus clear that the translational techniques involved in productions which are interventionist in the political and social sense and which necessarily involve aesthetic repositioning and cultural exchange are particularly controversial to critics and audiences, and that responses are likely to be conditioned by perceptions of cultural identity and ideological standpoint.[16] This means that in a situation of cultural and/or political conflict the role of interventionist theatre in transforming cultural perspectives may be uneven in scope and jerky in its progress. Only over a period of time is it possible to judge the extent to which what is judged to be innovatory or subversive in one context then attains the status of a translational norm.

In the chapters which follow I shall explore the impact and processes of translation as critical intervention in three modern contexts. The first is the situation of modern Irish writers' reworking of classical literature, and here the focus will be on the work of Seamus Heaney and its critical reception.The second is the post-colonial literature of the Caribbean with special reference to Derek Walcott's deployment of the figure of Philoctetes in his new epic poem *Omeros*. The third modern area which has increased in importance during the century is that of genre cross-over. I shall discuss Tony Harrison's *Prometheus* and two stage versions of the *Odyssey* as different kinds of encounter between ancient and modern, involving an encounter of genres as well as one of verbal and theatrical translational relationships.

5

Translation and Cultural Politics: The Irish Dimension

Help me to please my hedge-schoolmaster Virgil
And the child that's due. Maybe, heavens, sing
Better times for her and her generation.
                    Seamus Heaney, 'Bann Valley Eclogue'[1]

The relationship between modern Irish literature and classical texts intersects with most of the issues addressed in the chapters immediately preceding and following this one, but it does not entirely replicate any of them. Indeed, because of the special relationship in the Irish contexts between ideas about translation, tradition, identity, aesthetics and cultural politics, the role of classical texts and referents as catalysts for debate is unique. The dynamics of the debate also act as a useful check on temptations to generalise about the theory and practice of translational relationships, for instance in post-colonial literatures or in interventionist writing. That Seamus Heaney could address Vergil as his 'hedge-schoolmaster' and so invoke the image of teachers who were both classicists and nationalists, brings us directly into the intricacies of the exchanges between ancient and modern, dominant and marginalised, imperialist and colonised. The borders between these spheres and the assumptions that establish and guard those borders are constantly shifting. The cultural politics of the debates surrounding translations and the shifts in norms which they reveal hinge on changing perceptions of fidelity, equivalence and appropriation. These open up the whole question of the kinds of cultural operations which are involved when writing moves across the borders between the cultural authority of the ancient text and the modern positions and practices with which translation must engage. In this chapter I shall consider: first, the main features of perceptions about translation in Irish culture; secondly, the critical debates prompted by late twentieth-century literary engagement with classical texts; thirdly, the translational relationship between one influential example and its Greek source.

In the last quarter of the twentieth century the politics of translation has become the central issue in literary debate about Irish writers' use of classical referents. The debate ranges from questions about the interpretation and refiguring of particular works to broader questions about the cultural authority of the languages involved.

In Ireland translation has always been a crucial activity (Cronin 1996). This is partly because Irish culture has developed in and through interaction between the Irish language and other European languages, including 'dead' languages such as Latin, as well as with English and various kinds of Irish-English. Sometimes these relationships have been interactive and creative, sometimes they involve collision. Commentators have been swift to point out the association between (i) the long indigenous tradition of translation from Gaelic into Irish-English, with the resulting literature responding to the genius of both languages and even 'effecting a form of reconciliation that is far in advance of political reality' (Paulin, 1984, p. 214) and (ii) the more recent interest in translating classical and European poetry into Irish-English.

My contention is that, in respect both of translation issues (linguistic and cultural) and of the broad picture of historical and cultural conflict in Ireland, classical texts have played a crucial role both as indicators of attitudes and as catalysts for reformulation of debates and identities. As Robert Welch put it, 'the past is dangerous; ruins can fall on you ... [but] if a story is told as if it were happening again ... telling a story like this is translating it ... all legitimate intellectual enquiry is translation of one kind or another: it takes a text, a phase of history, an event, an instant of recognition and proceeds to understand it by reliving it in the process of recreating it' (Welch, 1993, pp. x-xi). For Welch, translation is 'the carrying over of the depth of association'. So within the modern Irish tradition there is an acceptance that iconic figures (such as the hero Cu Chulainn) are reconstructed, adapted and refigured in different ways. This refiguration is not necessarily regarded as appropriation (let alone colonising) but as a pointer either to continuity and overlap or to fracture and discontinuity (Deane, 1991, introduction). Within such a tradition there is special emphasis on the cultural activity and fluidity of translation, founded on notions of recovery, conversion, adaptation and transplantation rather than on the more limiting concept of fidelity. There is also an acceptance that translation can give a role to 'invented texts' (as in the work of James Clarence Mangan in the nineteenth century) and, by extension, to 'translations' of mythologies and other cultural constructs. Thus the idea of imaginative working across cultural borders precedes more recent concerns with political ones. Both notions of borders come together, as we shall see, in the reactions of critics to particular modern works.

The linguistic and political contours of these debates have been mapped by Brian Friel in his play *Translations* (1980). This was one of the first works created for the Field Day Theatre Company of Derry. Field Day took 'translation' both as its central focus and as an instrument for political change. The company's work has included versions of Greek plays (notably Tom Paulin's *The Riot Act*, 1984, based on Sophocles' *Antigone*, and Seamus Heaney's *The Cure at Troy*, 1990, which takes Sophocles' *Philoctetes* as its source text) but it also performs translations of Molière and Chekhov, and adaptations of English-language plays to Irish settings. The company's intention in interpreting non-Irish material for Ireland has been to provoke questions about the condition of Ireland in a way which would not be possible merely by staging 'standard' productions of canonical works.

Friel's play is set in the fictional community of Ballybeg, Co. Donegal, in 1833. It examines the effects on the community generated, first, by the Ordnance Survey which mapped and surveyed Ireland and translated Irish place names into English and, secondly, by the introduction of a system of 'national schools' which educated Irish-speaking children entirely through the medium of English. This system was intended to supersede the 'hedge-schools', held in rural barns or sheds. The 'hedge-schools' were a heritage of the penal laws in Ireland (*c.* 1690-1795) which forbade an official education for Catholic children. Greek and Latin literature were, according to tradition, a feature of hedge-schools. In the nineteenth century, Canon Sheehan is supposed to have said that 'The scholars took their sods of turf under their arms for school seats but every boy knew his Virgil and Horace and Homer as well as the last ballad about some rebel that was hanged' (quoted in Stanford, 1976, p. 27). Some scholars have questioned Friel's use of historical evidence in his play (both on the Survey and on National Schools) but there is certainly evidence in poems such as Padraic Colum's 'A Poor Scholar of the Forties' that the hedge-school's role in the collective literary memory preserves a tradition which combined classical education and critical questioning of the dominant regime.[2] Colum (1881-1972) was a folk lyricist from County Longford. More recent is the identification of Socrates with the hedge-school tradition in Desmond O'Grady's (b. 1935) 'Lines in a Roman Schoolbook'. The poem recalls a time when poets were hedge-school masters and

> ... kept alive
> the way of life that's ours by conversation –
> just as that other hedge-school master talked
> in his muddled market place under the Attic sun
> and paid the price extorted.

In Friel's play, Hugh (the hedge-schoolmaster) uses images from Vergil's account of the after-effects on the Greeks of the fall of Troy in an implicit analogy with British power in Ireland. Indeed, some critics have read the play as a whole as a covert allegory of the British Army's presence in the North of Ireland. However, the image of Troy as a touchstone for resistance to British domination certainly precedes by several centuries modern literary responses to military occupation. An early example is an anonymous epigram translated from the Irish in the eighteenth century which uses Troy as an icon of a power which can be swept away, as might be, by extension, the English:

> The world laid low, and the wind blew like a dust
> Alexander, Caesar, and all their followers.
> Tara is grass; and look how it stands with Troy
> And even the English – maybe they might die.[3]

Compare Pound's version of Agathias' epigram, cited in Chapter 3.

Another epigram also translated from the Irish in the eighteenth century makes a specific link between the suppression of both indigenous and ancient learning and consequent loss of political vigour:

5. Translation and Cultural Politics: The Irish Dimension

Loss of our learning brought darkness, weakness and woe
on me and mine, amid these unrighteous hordes.
Oafs have entered the places of the poets
and taken the light of the schools from everyone.[4]

Thus, we are faced with a view of the relationship between classical culture and the educational system which differs significantly from the model sometimes applied to colonised peoples, when a classical education might be seen as an alien system imposed by an imperial power to suppress indigenous culture and to promote assimilation of the colonised to the culture and values of the occupiers, rather than as a feature of pre-existing tradition valued by the oppressed. In Ireland classical learning was important before the Norman conquest, epic was translated into Irish from the late tenth century onwards and church reforms reflected the influence of the Cathedral schools of Northern France. This background of classical learning was important for the development of the universities (for example in Armagh). So not only was there interchange between the Irish and various invaders (pagans, Christian missionaries, Normans, pre-Reformation English, Elizabethans, Cromwellians and Williamites) but classical culture was rooted in Ireland, interacting with other strands, and was identified with independent critique, both aesthetic and political. No wonder that in the nineteenth century classical models and images continued to be important for Irish nationalists. It is significant that an otherwise relatively liberal Ascendancy figure, R.L. Edgeworth (father of the novelist), considered that the Irish education syllabus should prevent children learning about ancient Greece. He thought that even abridgements of ancient history for schools should be banned since 'to inculcate democracy and a foolish hankering after undefined liberty is not necessary in Ireland' (Letter to the Committee of the Board of Education, Parliamentary Papers 1813-14). The implication that knowledge of classical culture encouraged political independence was underlined when Thomas Davis argued that, while there was not time to learn the ancient languages, translations of key texts offered moral and political inspiration to nationalists (Address to the Trinity College Historical Society, 1840).

So in one way, Friel's play draws on a tradition in which knowledge of the ancient poets was a mark of an Irish education which offered icons and allegories for political debate. Classical referents could be a token of resistance. Yet in the play classical languages are also used as cultural bridges, as a means of getting Irish and English speakers, who cannot otherwise understand one another, to communicate. The hedge-schoolmaster Hugh sums up the apparent dichotomy which classical culture can represent: in one sense it is an icon of a past cultural authority, a monument imprisoning the minds of those who admire it uncritically, and yet it can also serve as a possible means of translating issues into newer contexts and of enabling communication across boundaries.

The sometimes uneasy relationship between these two possibilities underlies much of the critical debate about the viability in the Irish context of engagement with classical themes and texts. For those who accept the broad cultural aims associated with Field Day, it is clear that translations and versions of classical texts can help deliver the company's interventionist agenda, calling attention to the condition of Ireland (or at least the aspects of it privileged by Field Day). In this respect, classical poetry and drama are sources of artistic and cultural substance and energise work based on the creative and politically liberal associations of the classical tradition in Ireland. These associations have their origins in pre-Ascendancy intellectual and artistic influences and were developed to include education of and for ordinary people, including otherwise marginalised Catholics. Classical texts provided cultural icons amenable both to recuperation and to critique, and according to Friel's dramatisation provided a basis for creating cultural and political dialogue and transforming attitudes. This was possible because classical knowledge became part of the cultural traditions of social, religious and political group who might otherwise have found little common ground for cultural exchange, especially ground that was both accessible to them and yet also sufficiently distant from current ideologies not to be regarded as 'occupied' by any group.

These points are not unproblematic. Modern critical response to translations and revisions of classical sources has sometimes resisted the view that classical referents sharpen intervention and promote dialogue. Some critics argue that setting up equivalences between ancient and modern literature and drama is a negative activity, based either on nostalgia or, more dangerously, importing ancient religious and social frameworks into modern consciousness. An influential proponent of this view is Shaun Richards, who has analysed the impact of the forms and concepts of Greek tragedy on modern drama in Ireland (Richards 1995). He examines tragedy as both a descriptive term and a theatrical form and develops a critique of the modern practice of applying dramatic frameworks derived (directly or indirectly) from Greek tragedy to the situation of contemporary Ireland, especially the North. His view is derived partly from his reading, based on the fourth-century BCE discussion in Aristotle's *Poetics*, of what the concept of tragedy implies. Richards' emphasis is on the notion that tragedy involves the creation and communication of the emotions of pity and fear, which are eventually purged in the audience through the cathartic tragic climax to the action. Richards also takes a somewhat 'closed' view of the dominance of the Greek idea of destiny, interpreting this as implying a sense of inevitability which marginalises or even completely displaces the issue of human responsibility. Richards argues on this basis that both the ethos and the form of tragedy transplant the idea of inevitability into the situation in Northern Ireland, enabling the modern audience and performers to escape a sense of responsibility for current and future actions. In other words, the 'interventionist' impact of modern Irish translations of Greek drama would be negative, inspiring only resignation and failing to transform perspectives.

In support of his argument Richards focuses on a specific example, a TV film production *In the Border Country* (Channel 4, March 1991, directed by Thaddeus O'Sullivan). The film dramatises the killing of a returning IRA gunman by his neighbour in complicity with the gunman's wife, whom he subsequently marries. Both are in turn killed by the gunman's son. There are obvious and close affinities with the Greek myth of the house of Atreus in which Agamemnon is killed on his return to Argos from Troy by his wife Clytemnestra and her lover Aegisthus, who are then killed in revenge by Orestes, the son of Clytemnestra and Agamemnon. To explore these equivalences further, the TV film included screened quotations from Robert Fagles' translation of Aeschylus' trilogy *The Oresteia*, which had the effect of giving the drama a tripartite structure. Before the final sequence, the screened quotation was from the second play in Aeschylus' trilogy, *The Libation Bearers*:

> And the blood that mother Earth consumes
> clots hard, it won't seep through, it breeds revenge
> and frenzy goes through the guilty
> seething like infection, swarming through the brain

This eventually leads to the realisation that –

> It is the law: when the blood of slaughter
> Wets the ground, it wants more blood.

The issues raised range from specific points about the translation and semiotic context of the visual images to debate about how Greek tragedy communicates (through both form and content) and what and how it transplants into modern consciousness. Of course, as Richards acknowledges, the debate and action about compromise and reconciliation in the *Eumenides,* the final play of the *Oresteia* trilogy, were omitted from *In the Border Country*, which ended with the matricide. According to Richards' reading of the film, this left an implication of cultural and aesthetic sanctioning of an endless cycle of blood-letting and revenge as a kind of 'tragedy', which was to be seen as an inevitable part of the human destiny of Irish people. Thus the image of 'infection' could operate in two spheres, both in the source text and in the 'transfusion' of its imagery and energy into the modern film drama. Of course this then confronts us with the crucial question of how the plays are to be performed. Roland Barthes framed the questions thus: 'Are the Greek plays to be performed as of their own time or as of ours?' He thought that the historical specificity of the original context had to be grasped before it was possible to make dynamic use of it or to grasp a sense of the movement of history, especially of the way in which art can be thought to intervene in history and even change the world. The implication of this view is that, paradoxically, it is only when the alienating and distancing impact of Greek tragedy is felt by the writer, players and audience that its involvement in modern dilemmas can be explored and understood.

While Richards' view that the Greek strand in modern Irish drama and film is a negative contribution to Intervention seems to me to be misplaced, his criticisms do serve the very useful purpose of provoking readers and audience to re-examine the relationship between the new work and the source text. The critic George Steiner has urged that a poetic dramatist must write within the context of a pattern of belief shared by the audience (Steiner, 1980, pp. 303-24). In lamenting the 'death of tragedy' Steiner identified shared patterns of belief as one of three criteria which would have to be met if poetic drama were to have any future. His other two criteria are that modern poetry has to *impose* itself in the theatre (Steiner thinks poetry has become too intimate) and that poetry has to regain its power of meaning and mystery (lost, he thinks, in the twentieth century because of abuse by agents of political terror and by the illiteracy implicit in mass consumption). There seems to be some contradiction in practice between the first and third criteria.

Analysis of the range of translations and versions of Greek drama created by Irish writers in the last twenty years suggests that tragedy is not dead and also reveals a multiplicity of approaches and a wide choice of source plays. Since 1984 twelve translations/adaptations of Greek tragedies have been created by Irish writers. They are listed below with their Greek sources:

Sophocles: *Antigone*	Tom Paulin: *The Riot Act* (1984)
	Aidan Carl Mathews: *Antigone* (1984)
	Brendan Kennelly: *Antigone* (1985)
Euripides: *The Bacchae*	Derek Mahon: *The Bacchae* (1991)
Euripides: *Iphigenia in Aulis*	Colin Teevan: *Iph* (1996)
Sophocles: *Electra*	Frank McGuinness: *Electra* (1997)
Euripides: *Medea*	Brendan Kennelly: *Medea* (1991)
	Desmond Egan: *Medea* (1991: a close translation)
Sophocles: *Philoctetes*	Seamus Heaney: *The Cure at Troy* (1990)
[Aeschylus]: *Prometheus Bound*	Tom Paulin: *Seize the Fire* (1989)
Euripides: *Women of Troy*	Aidan Carl Mathews: *Trojans* (1994)
	Brendan Kennelly: *The Trojan Women* (1993)

To these may be added Paul Muldoon's version of Aristophanes' comedy *Birds* (1999). *Prometheus, Antigone* and *Medea* figure prominently and indicate a focus on resistance to unjust authority figures. Nevertheless, it is clear from the range of plays and from individual treatments that it is not the case that writers have focussed entirely on the oppositions of Britain/Ireland and coloniser/colonised. Other aspects of Irish identity have also been examined, for example constructions of gender and the impact of social change. Even when the choice of play and its translation/adaptation directly raise issues of political authority and resistance, there is sometimes a further level of distancing from present concerns. For example, Aidan Carl Mathew's *Trojans* (1994), based on Euripides' *Women of Troy*, is set in Berlin in 1945 and explores the effects of war and religious conflict with reference to Nazi Germany, thus further deferring direct links with the situation in Ireland. Critical reaction to these translations and adaptations gives the lie to claims about the élitist and limited interest of classical revivals. In fact, one tranche of criticism has been that the new cycle of adaptations is not academic enough. Critics who resist the view that the upsurge in literary and theatrical interest in Greek drama represents a post-colonial cultural project have argued that the plays are being 'mis-translated' and that the formal and cultural ethos of the Greek is being forced into an allegorical relationship with current political concerns (including gender issues as well as sectarian politics) which exaggerates the political potential of translational practices (O'Rawe 2000).

This aspect of the debate was triggered by various attempts in the 1980s to appropriate Sophocles' *Antigone* to the conflict between Nationalists and Unionists in Northern Ireland. It was also informed by the controversy generated in 1968 by Conor Cruise O'Brien concerning the contemporary resonances of Sophocles' play and especially the possible equivalence of Antigone's stand with the civil rights protests led, among others, by the young activist Bernadette Devlin. Tom Paulin's *The Riot Act* (1984) has sometimes been interpreted as a challenge to O'Brien's attempt to defend the practicality and morality of Creon's stance on behalf of public order against Antigone's disruption. Paulin's rendering of Creon's key speech on this issue seems to mirror the thoughts of 'public men' at any time and in any place, but it is expressed in the idiom and register of Ulster/Irish/English. However, by the 1980s the possibility of direct political equivalence was not the only issue. Also important were examination of the linguistic and poetic strategies involved in 'translating' the situation and the dilemmas involved and the question of the relationship between feminist and republican standpoints in Antigone's opposition to Creon.

More complex is the treatment of Sophocles' *Antigone* in the film *Anne Devlin* (1984, directed by Pat Murphy), which is based on the story of Robert Emmet's housekeeper in the 1803 rebellion and involves a re-reading of women's place in Irish history and society. In the film, Anne Devlin exhumes from an unmarked grave the corpse of a United Irishman which is then taken in a cart drawn by women for burial with Catholic rites in his own community, despite the intervention of British redcoats. But the impact is to create a double consciousness. Anne also calls Republican ideals into question by exposing the patriarchal principles on which they were constructed (Roche, 1988).

More recently, the play that has provoked the greatest debate about the representation of equivalence between ancient and modern situations is Seamus Heaney's version of Sophocles' *Philoctetes, The Cure at Troy* (1990). Arguably, of all modern poets, the 1995 Nobel Laureate Heaney was the most likely to succeed in adapting Greek tragedy to modern theatre in a way that would both meet Steiner's three criteria for poetic tragedy and walk the tightrope between political engagement and audience expectations of theatricality with which theatre in Ireland (and elsewhere) has to contend.

Heaney's initial choice of the *Philoctetes* and his approach to the adaptation develop parallels between the experience of the individual poet and the experience of leaders in a community facing change. In a letter Heaney has referred to 'a fascination with the conflict between the integrity of the personal bond and the exactions of the group's demands for loyalty. A sense that the pride in the wound is stronger that the desire for a cure ... the intoxication of defiance over the civic, sober path of adjustment' (quoted in McDonald, 1996). In an early poem, 'Digging' (in *Death of a Naturalist*, 1966), Heaney grappled with the issue of the cultural and political status of the artist:

> Between my finger and my thumb
> The squat pen rests; snug as a gun.

Heaney's pen may be a weapon, like the bow of Philoctetes, and like Philoctetes he has been seen by some as an exile (from the North) and unwilling to use his weapon and lend his support to the achievement of victory for his community through violence. In referring also to the 'culture of narcissism, victim-pride kind of daemon that is rampant at the moment', his letter about *The Cure at Troy* also addresses the problem of the wound, of the pride in affliction and in being oppressed (with which Derek Walcott also contends), and his 'I sort of liked the golden mean talk of Heracles at the end of the play' presages the longing for peace and hope that he went on to picture in his poem 'Bann Valley Eclogue' 1999.

Yet Heaney has also used classical sources to explore the ambivalent relationship between peace and victory, choosing to focus again on the image of Troy and its cultural associations in 'Mycenae Lookout', the dominant poem in his 1996 collection *The Spirit Level*. The poem is headed by a quotation from Aeschylus'*Agamemnon*, 'The ox is on my tongue' and is in five sections: The Watchman's war; Cassandra; His dawn vision; The Nights; and finally His Reverie of Water, a vision of water polluted by blood which links Troy, Athens and 'the ladder of the future'. The watchman in the poem tries to apply himself to his task:

> Exposed to what I knew, still honour-bound
> To concentrate attention out beyond
> The city and the border, on that line
> Where the blaze would leap the hills when Troy had
>   fallen.

Yet his concentration is shattered by nightmares –

> ... and I would feel my tongue
> Like the dropped gangplank of a cattle truck
> Trampled and rattled, running piss and muck,
> All swimmy-trembly as the lick of fire,
> A victory beacon in an abattoir ...

The echo of the language of slaughter from Aeschylus and the resonance with twentieth-century genocide (to which Tony Harrison also responded both visually and verbally in his film *Prometheus*; see Chapter 8 below), leave the poet/watchman/observer:

> ... balanced between destiny and dread
> And saw it coming, clouds bloodshot with the red
> Of victory fires, the raw wound of that dawn
> Igniting and erupting bearing down
> Like lava on a fleeing population ...

Destiny and dread: a reminder of Owen's bleak conclusion that all the poet can do is warn.

The raw wound and the sense of destiny and dread frame *The Cure at Troy*. At a first reading of the printed text, the structure and content of Heaney's play seem remarkably close to the Greek source. The play is actually subtitled 'after *Philoctetes* by Sophocles'. The description 'after' applies in two different ways. The play indeed follows the Sophoclean plot outline and the imagery of the wound with its pain, poison, decay and psychological effects. It also follows the Greek conventions, especially the chorus' role as commentator, moral interpreter and guide to the action. It uses, too, the Greek poetical forms which frame the engagements between the actors, especially the *agon* or confrontational debate between major characters and the *stichomythia* or line-by-line dialogue which sharpens the debate and rattles like arrows or bullets on the hearing and minds of the spectators. It also closely replicates the confusing pattern of ethical choice and uncertainty about the disentangling of the true and the false in human relationships with which Sophocles' play is concerned.

Yet of course the play is also 'after' Sophocles in the sense that its performance is filtered through the poet's, actors', director's and spectators' consciousness of what has intervened between the Athens of the fifth century BCE and the late twentieth century. Aspects of this consciousness are signalled by the design and production style for a play which has been well travelled ever since its opening tour by the Field Day Theatre Company. For example, in the production at the Lyric Players Theatre, Belfast, in October 1990 the opening set suggested the play's ambivalent relationship to modern perceptions of Greek drama by having a white sheet covering everything on the stage. This billowed up to reveal the fragmented head of a white Greek sculpture. In 1999 in the productions at the Edinburgh Festival Fringe and the Oxford Playhouse, both directed by Helen Eastman, the emphasis from the beginning was on modern resonances, with the opening sequence staged as a student bar argument.

The core of Heaney's translational technique is, however, to use the Greek conventions to move the action into the consciousness of the receiving audience, rather than to use the Greek conventions to move the audience into the distant world of the Greeks. This tone is set from the opening Chorus which (in contrast to Neoptolemus' sailors in *Philoctetes*) consists of three women (sometimes in practice played as a mixed male/female Chorus), who, in preparing the way for the entry of Odysseus and Neoptolemus, also introduce the Sophoclean critique of the rigidity and hardness which is an explicit part of the heroic tradition. The Sophoclean allusions to the quarrel between Achilles and Agamemnon and to Homer's *Iliad* book 2 are translated into modern idiom:

> People are so deep into
> their own self-pity   self-pity buoys them up.
> People so staunch and true, they're fixated,
> Shining with self-regard like polished stones.
>   … Licking their wounds
> And flashing them around like decorations.
>
>

The Cure at Troy, pp. 1-2

This confrontation opens the way for members of the audience to pick up the resonances for their own society and to establish their own connection to the play. Some critics have been unambiguous in their perception of the equivalences, for example 'sullen, rancorous, inwardly gnawed by hatred and paralysed by memories of past injustice, Philoctetes is Heaney's unlovely image of the sectarian North of Ireland' (Eagleton, 1991).

Even more detailed modern equivalences can be imagined, although it seems rather an arid occupation to debate whether the play more directly invokes the unionist rather than the nationalist community, or can be read as presaging the (later) debates about the decommissioning of terrorist arms. Sophocles' play has in any case been staged and adapted in other political contexts, for instance in the GDR in

5. Translation and Cultural Politics: The Irish Dimension

Heiner Müller's adaptation (see Chapter 4) or indeed in the context of the alienation caused by unemployment in Belfast in 1933 when the performance was regarded as a useful occupation and fundraiser for the jobless. The crucial question has not been one of narrow appropriation of Heaney's play to any particular cause, but rather whether his translational strategies for establishing modern resonances are aesthetically flawed. He himself wrote in the 1991 Programme Notes for the production at the Tricycle Theatre Kilburn: 'I have done this play in verse in order to preserve something of the formal ritualistic quality of the Greek theatrical experience; at the same time ... [I] felt free to compose a number of new lines for the Chorus.'

These 'new lines' are used to introduce specific modern analogues of suffering inflicted within and across communities, for instance –

> A hunger striker's father
> Stands in the graveyard dumb
> The police widow in veils
> Faints at the funeral home
> *The Cure at Troy*, p. 77

The lines have been described as 'intrusively overt' or even as part of an attempt to create 'a new mythology' (Meir, 1991) and significantly were omitted from the recitation of the Choral ode by Liam Neeson for *Across the Bridge of Hope* (1998), a compilation album produced in aid of the Omagh Bomb Memorial Fund. Such specific references were also cut from a production in the United States in 1995 since Heaney felt: 'I'm not sure I should have mentioned hunger strikers and police ... I remember feeling it was like a puncture ... Nowhere else is there Northern Ireland local reference, and it's just as if you've pumped the whole play up and then, at the last minute, pssht! the tension goes out' (quoted in Wilmer, 1999). However, even with such deletions it is not true to say that there is no local reference. The language in which Heaney explores the situation of Philoctetes is resonant with Irish-English because that is his idiom.

It is, perhaps, the final Chorus of Heaney's play which has been most remarked –

> Once in a lifetime
> The longed for tidal wave
> Of justice can rise up
> And hope and history rhyme
> So hope for a great sea change
> On the far side of revenge.
>
> *The Cure at Troy*, p. 77

'Hope and history rhyme' has become almost a cultural cliché since its appropriation by newspaper headlines at the time of the Good Friday Agreement (Belfast 1998). Critics have pointed out the ambivalent relationship between these lines and the fact that sacking Troy was itself an act of revenge. I suspect that Heaney's initial strategy of using the Chorus to deliver specific guidance to the modern resonances of the play was determined by his view of the likely audiences for the Field Day Tour. A major aim of the Company is to take theatre to people who might not have much opportunity for theatregoing. One of the performances was in a parish hall in Andersonstown, a working class Republican area of Belfast. For most of the audience there, unlike the participants in the hedge-schools, knowledge of classical sources was probably not a part of their cultural horizons. Therefore, additional translational techniques were required to assist that shift of understanding and imagination which interventionist theatre requires. Perhaps the broader audience, whether in Ireland, UK or USA, felt more comfortable with the message of hope and did not want to be reminded that the infection resulting from affliction and from sectarian bigotry is not peculiar to one country. As a poem, perhaps the *Cure at Troy* needed the specific referents; to achieve success as a play, design and staging could have been allowed to focus the audience's awareness more subtly according to the actors' and director's sense of the equivalences between ancient and modern which Heaney's play suggests. For any kind of audience, Sophocles' central thrust that Neoptolemus recognises a duty to someone in a liminal place, exiled from the life of the community, is translated by Heaney into recognition of a duty towards outsiders. Sophocles and Heaney share the ethos that it is poetry not rhetoric which can communicate this sense of obligation. For those who know the narrative outside the play, awareness of Neoptolemus' acts of sacrilege and butchery at Troy clouds the horizon. Like the Mycenae Lookout, we are balanced between a sense of destiny and a sense of dread.

6

Walcott's Philoctete: Imaging the Post-Colonial Condition

... I grew tired, like wounded Philoctetes,
the hermit who did not know the war was over,
or refused to believe it.
                    Walcott, *Omeros* book 4.XXXIII.II p. 171

Heaney's version of Sophocles' play kept closely to the language and connections of Greek tragedy and in so doing kept beneath the surface the association between the archer and the poet. Because of the close relationship between Heaney's play and its Greek source, Heaney's Philoctetes retained the heroic associations exploited by Sophocles, while also drawing on 'the particular twist', in Edmund Wilson's words, that Sophocles gave to the myth.[1] Sophocles' other plays also display his interest in people such as Electra and Ajax, whose attitudes and personalities have been poisoned by narrow and fanatical hatreds, who suffer and hate in return but in so doing nevertheless arouse understanding and pity. It was that 'twist' which made Heaney's version so relevant and so contentious in the context of modern Ireland.

In Derek Walcott's long poem *Omeros*, a new epic in conception, content and range, the figure of Philoctetes is transplanted into a cultural context which is obviously different both from the Greek myth and its adaptation in tragedy and from the political context and literary tradition in which Heaney explored its significance. Yet there are, too, significant links both with the Greek sources (epic and tragic) and with the Irish context. The links with the Greek sources are identified and expressed through formal conventions. Those with the Irish context are derived from correspondences (though not congruity) in post-colonial and post-imperial situations. They emerge through

97

the ambivalence in the identity of the Philoctetes figure and in the poet's resolution of pain, suffering and intransigence – the means of 'cure'. Both Walcott's and Heaney's translations of the figure of Philoctetes are shaped by elements in Greek myth and literature; their differences point not only to differences in the Caribbean and Irish contexts but also to the multifaceted possibilities in the Greek sources.

Walcott has often denied that *Omeros* is an epic poem in the strict sense – 'I do not think of it as an epic ... that isn't the Homer I was thinking of' (*New York Times*, 9 October 1990); 'The theme of the book is not really a parallel, an overlay, putting the *Iliad* or the *Odyssey* over a village in the Caribbean' (*Poetry Please*, 20 October 1990). Indeed, he has claimed never to have finished reading the *Iliad* and the *Odyssey*: 'the gods get in the way' (interview at the Hay-on-Wye Literary Festival, May 1991). Yet in its scope and multi-layered structure *Omeros* is certainly of epic proportions. It has 64 chapters, each of which is divided into sections. Some of these sections are as short as nine lines, others are nearly one hundred lines. The whole is organised into seven books, although the length of the books is nowhere near uniform. The lines are usually grouped in threes with a rhyme scheme that operates across alternate lines (sometimes with half rhymes). This resembles the *terza rima* used by Dante in *The Divine Comedy*.[2]

Omeros can be described as a modern epic not merely because it is a long poem but because it is structured round interlocked layers of meaning. It is also, as Walcott's own comments suggest, a poem of paradoxes. It is laced with allusions to and echoes of canonical texts (Homer, Vergil, Dante) and framed by the grand themes of imperialism and diaspora (in this case the displacement of Africans to the Caribbean through enslavement, of Europeans to the Caribbean by commerce and Empire, and of the narrator from his island through education, poetry and political conflict). Yet it communicates these ideas through the images and vernacular of popular culture. Thus, paradoxically, this poem represents a diaspora of the classical canon itself, which is both decentred from European cultural hegemony and then refreshes and is refreshed by the decolonised cultures it encounters.

The translational techniques involved in the creation of this new epic operate at several levels. The basic indicators are names. The Caribbean community imagined in the poem includes, as well as

6. Walcott's Philoctete: Imaging the Post-Colonial Condition

Philoctete, another poor fisherman (Achille), an upwardly-mobile taxi driver (Hektor), a beautiful waitress (Helen) and a blind ex-seaman Seven Seas, the Omeros of the poem. Helen is not only the 'cause' of a quarrel between Achille and Hektor but also the 'prize' for which the athletes compete in the informal games pictured in chapter VI. Here Walcott uses a double simile to signal a double perspective, but a perspective viewed from the islanders' standpoint:

> As in your day, so with ours, Omeros
> as it is with the islands and men, so with our games ...
> *Omeros* book 1.VI.I p. 33

Men competed and fought for the islands of the Caribbean and St. Lucia; Walcott's own island was known historically as the Helen of the Caribbean, representing, like women in the poem, a 'true bounty'.

So the use of the simile becomes the pivotal translational mechanism. The poem is not a direct retelling of episodes from Homer, even in the context of a different culture. Indeed, Walcott undercuts most expectations on the part of the reader who has detailed knowledge of Homer. Although Walcott exploits Greek associations to include within the life and language of the poem names, relationships and situations familiar from Homer, even the names have a double-edged resonance, bringing with them reminders of the plantation culture which replaced the African names of its slaves with classical ones. The poet's reference to 'All that Greek manure under the green bananas' (book 6.LIV.III p. 271) signals the ambivalent relationship between cultural enrichment and its association with the classical culture that arrived with empire and is thus associated with its 'heritage' of slavery and imperialism. In the same way, his use of Greek names opens up similes suggesting relationships between ancient and modern, rather than simplifying and closing identities.

In the poem as a whole the formal device of the simile becomes, in Walcott as in Homer, a vehicle through which the audience (readers) understand a text which explores social values and contexts far removed from their own experience. In provoking the readers to engage with a web of insights and relationships in the poem, Walcott's similes also stimulate them to engage with and move on from the limitations of their expectations and assumptions. This is a process of perspective transformation. This translates the process (although not, of course, the content) which takes place in the Homeric epics, where the simile, which operates as a poetic technique with a formal and structural role within the poems, also influences and creates shifts in the imaginative response of the audience. (I use the term audience rather than readers since the Homeric epics are part of a performance culture, derived from a long oral tradition.) Studies of the Homeric simile have shown how these range from short similes used to characterise particular figures, actions or natural features to various kinds of long simile, the most complex of which introduce a new idea which is then carried into the narrative. The most effective similes refer both forwards and backwards so that they provide an underlying framework for the structural development of the poem.[3]

The long simile in Homer takes the audience away from the poem and improvises on experiences and allusions external to the poem. The experience and cultural standpoint of the audience are caught, and as the formal elements of the simile return it to the poem, the members of the audience internalise the processes and emotions described in the poem through the filter of their own experiences, which they then bring to their further reading of the poem. The simile, therefore, both differentiates and connects. The connection may also link apparently disparate communities of understanding. In Walcott, the formal aspects of the simile are sometimes simply signalled by following the Homeric pattern 'as ... so', as in the example concerning the games, quoted above. More frequently the simile relationship with Homer is introduced by allusion. There is a good example in the opening lines of the poem in which Philoctete recounts:

> This is how, one sunrise, we cut down them canoes

He goes on to describe, in a pastiche of heroic action, how they cut down the trees to provide timber for the canoes. The workmen wound the trees, like killers. The images draw on the Homeric simile in the *Iliad* when Homer describes the killing of Sarpedon, by Patroclus:

> He fell, as when an oak goes down or a white poplar
> or like a towering pine tree which in the mountains the carpenters

have hewn down with their whetted axes to make a ship-timber.
So he lay there felled.
Iliad 16.482-5, trans. R.L. Lattimore

The effect of the allusion is two-fold. First, mastery over the harvest
from trees is given a quasi-heroic status, and secondly, from this is
derived status for the fishermen. Walcott's poetic treatment of the
episode is tragi-comic, but its significance is rooted in Homer's juxtaposition through simile of the status of the hero and the experiences
of the peasant.

The Caribbean context makes Philoctete not a hero but an object of
cultural curiosity to outsiders:

> Philoctete smiles for the tourists who try taking
> his soul with their cameras

The ambiguity of the words 'taking his soul' alerts the readers to the
cultural and social threat, and this theme is developed by a further
allusion to the Philoctetes myth:

> For some extra silver, under a sea-almond,
> he shows them a scar made by a rusted anchor ...
> *Omeros* book 1.I.I p.4

The Greek hero Philoctetes' wound was caused by a snake bite. In
Homer's *Iliad* 2.718-23 we are told that:

> ... he himself lay apart in the island, suffering strong pains
> in Lemnos, the sacrosanct, where the sons of the Achaians had
> left him in
> agony from the sore bite of the wicked water snake ...
> trans. R.L. Lattimore

As the water snake was to Philoctetes, so was the rusty anchor to
Philoctete. In *Omeros*, as in the *Cure at Troy,* the wound becomes a
metaphor for the history and social and moral dilemmas of a community. The rusted anchor which caused the infection in Philoctete's
wound activates a sequence of images which map out a Caribbean

101

significance for the metaphor. The anchor suggests the ships of conquerors and slavers; rust spreads infection at a touch.[4] Eventually Philoctete is cured by the African herbal remedies given by the wise-woman Ma Kilman:

> She bathed him in the brew of the root. The basin
> was one of those cauldrons from the old sugar-mill ...
> She had one in her back yard, close to the crotons,
> agape in its crusted agonised O: the scream
> of centuries ...
> 　　　The lime leaves leeched to his wet
> knuckled spine like islands that cling to the basin
> of the rusted Caribbean ...
> 　　　　... he could feel the putrescent skin
> drain in the seethe like sucked marrow, he felt it drag
> the slime from his shame ...
> and as he surrendered to her, the foul flower
> on his skin whitened and puckered, the corolla
> closed its thorns like the sea-egg. What else did it cure?
> 　　　　　　　　*Omeros* book 6.XLIX.I pp. 246-7

Walcott answers the question metaphorically in the section which immediately follows:

> The bow leapt back to the palm of the warrior.
> The yoke of the wrong name lifted from his shoulders.
> His muscles loosened like those of a brown river
> that was dammed with silt and then silkens its boulders
> with refreshing strength.
> 　　　　　　　　*Omeros* book 6.XLIX.II p. 247

The cure is not, however, confined to the fisherman Philoctete. The wound caused by the rusty anchor activates a metaphor of pain and healing, both individual and social. Already in the poem the pain and sense of alienation from the community have been shared with the anonymous narrator, the 'I' of the poem. 'I' is a Walcott-like figure who has his roots in St. Lucia but has become alienated from the community and has moved on. When Philoctete waves to him, 'I' realises that 'we shared the one wound, the same cure' (book 7.LIX..I p. 295). Since the narrator's wound is psychological and moral, not physical, his cure actually involves a process of enlightenment and self-recovery rather than being a response to a herbal cure remedy. His cure is multi-layered (Hardwick, 1997). At one level, he recovers from a love affair with a character called Circe who charmed and delighted him and caused him to perceive himself as a pig. As with Odysseus' sojourn with Circe in Homer's *Odyssey* the narrator's love affair both delays his re-discovery of his home island and yet represents a necessary part of his journey towards self-awareness. In *Omeros*, self-awareness follows realisation that History as taught to the islanders fulfilled a Circe-like role, deluding them into accepting oppression and exploitation. Most painful of all is the part of the cure at which the narrator-poet realises that language, too, can cause Circe-like delusions and anchor-like wounds; it can become an agent of human manipulation. Yet this language, in the form of poetry, also enabled the narrator to imagine and explore the feelings and inner lives of the members of his community. Poetry could wound but 'like Philoctete's wound .... Carries its cure, its radiant affliction' (book 7.LXIV.II p. 323) Like Philoctetes' arrows, the power of the narrator's poetry could not be permanently marooned on an island.

The wounding dynamics of Caribbean history and politics and the dilemma of a creative intellectual who both is and is not a part of his own community are directly addressed in Walcott's autobiographical poem *Another Life*.[5] This anticipates the metaphors and structural similes in *Omeros* in its devastating attack on those who 'chafe and nurture the scars of rusted chains – they measure each other's sores to boast who has suffered most' (*Another Life*, Ch. 19, Frescoes of the New World II). In *Omeros,* however, the mature poet has created a narrator who reflects on a wider process of wounding and curing in which Greek allusions have the shaping role. The poetics of the poem are developed from an interplay of similes, names and metaphors which activate a dialogue between the experiences and insights of ancient Greek and modern western and Caribbean cultures.

Yet Walcott's characterisation of the rusty anchor of past oppressions as a source of poison in the present and as an obstacle to future development (whether political, social or poetic) is controversial. So, too, is his choice of Greek images as a mechanism for developing his analysis and critique of his own society. He has criticised other modern Caribbean writers for being absorbed in 'self-pity', 'rage' and 'masochistic recollection' and reiterated his opposition to an African-Caribbean literature which concentrates only on the suffering of the victim.[6] Walcott's alternative is to create a celebration of the potential of the African of the New World, stimulated by a condition of perpetual exile and growing within a context of shared diaspora alongside and intermingled with other cultural traditions. It is this hybrid nature which Walcott proclaims on an individual as well as on a more generalised level. The words of Shabine in *The Schooner Flight* are emblematic:

> I'm just a red nigger who love the sea,
> I had a sound colonial education.
> I have Dutch, nigger and English in me,
> And either I'm nobody or I'm a nation.
>> Walcott, *Collected Poems 1948-1984*
>> (1986) p. 346

In the mature work *Omeros*, Walcott is able both to recognise the historical and emotional force of the wounds of slavery and imperial exploitation and to move beyond them. Philoctete's wound may be caused by the slave-past of his people, but it is also exacerbated by continuing material poverty after emancipation:

> He believed the swelling came from the chained ankles
> of his grandfathers. Or else why was there no cure?
> That the cross he carried was not only the anchor's
> but that of his race, for a village black and poor
> as the pigs that rooted in its burning garbage,
> then were hooked on the anchors of the abattoir.
>> *Omeros* book 1.III.III p. 19

The combination of half simile and intratextual allusion carries the implication that it is not only the history of slavery but also the impact of poverty that makes 'pigs' of people (in the sense both of being poor and of being enslaved by Circe and her control of 'History'). Even after his cure, Philoctete can still feel the pain:[7]

104

6. Walcott's Philoctete: Imaging the Post-Colonial Condition

> All the pain
> re-entered Philoctete, of the hacked yams, the hold
> closing over their heads, the bolt-closing iron,
> over eyes that never saw the light of this world
>
> *Omeros* book 6.LV.III p. 277

Yet the poem also denies the uniqueness of the suffering experienced by the colonised and enslaved. It is not only Philoctete, the descendant of slaves, who is wounded but also Plunkett, the descendant of slavers:

> This wound I have stitched into Plunkett's character
> He has to be wounded, affliction is one theme
> of this work
>
> *Omeros* book 1.V.II p. 28

Furthermore, the name Philoctete associates the Caribbean fisherman not with slavery but with victory, with emergence from suffering and eventual triumph and, even more important, with the necessity and dignity ascribed to the Greek Philoctetes' role with his bow in the fall of Troy. The Philoctetes image and the translational mechanisms for energising it within the poem together represent an assertion of the hybrid vitality of a post-colonial literature that has emerged not only from the fetters of the past but also from pressures of the past in the present and now celebrates a confident and autonomous sense of cultural identity. Walcott's response to the poetry of affliction has been described as one of an astonishing hybridity that exemplifies the cross-cultural fabric of post-colonial poetry and contravenes the widespread assumption that post-colonial literature develops by sloughing off Eurocentrism (Ramazani, 1997, p. 405).

This however, is achieved only painfully, and in the poem the reconstruction of the process as a whole is completed in an ironic episode of *katabasis* (descent to the underworld). The *katabasis* is an epic convention through which the visitor to the underworld is guided into a re-examination of the past and its figures and through this achieves a wisdom informed by hindsight (for example, in *Odyssey* 2 Odysseus is enabled to view the afterlife of the great heroes Agamemnon and Achilles). In *Omeros*, Walcott transplants and adapts this poetic tradition in order to examine and question the cultural force of the African roots of Caribbean people.

The descent narrative is part of *Omeros* book 3. Achille, a poor fisherman but a dominant figure in the society of the poem, makes an imagined return voyage to Africa (*Omeros* book 3.XXV-XXVIII). The sequence alludes to a number of journeys of discovery in ancient epic, including not only Odysseus' Descent to the Underworld in Homer's *Odyssey* 2, but also to Vergil's *Aeneid* 8 in which Aeneas, the displaced survivor from the ruins of Troy, makes a journey up the river Tiber to visit Evander and discovers a model Greek colony in which the reasons and justifications for conquest are explained to him. Walcott also borrows from Dante's *Divine Comedy* not only the *terza rima* verse form but also the half-detached authorial voice, standing back from the action but engaged with it. There is a startling virtuosity in Walcott's improvisation on images which carry multiple resonances. For example, the image of the prow of the canoe as it nuzzles into the shore is likened to a piglet searching for the sow's dug. Striking in itself, the metaphor also undercuts Vergil's image of the sources of Rome's power (in *Aeneid* 8) and associates it with the theme in *Omeros* that 'Empires were swinish' thus linking the passage with the poem's structural emblem of the pig as a symbol of enslavement to Circe, whom he also associates with the seductive power of history.

In the descent to the underworld in Homer, Anticleia fails to recognise her son Odysseus. The equivalent in *Omeros* is that Achille's 'father' in Africa, Afolabe, is represented as having forgotten the name he gave him. He then asks about Achille's new name and its meaning. Although 'Time translates' (book 3.XXV.III p. 137), Achille is more and more conscious of his displacement:

> The deaf sea has changed around every name that you gave
> us; trees, men, we yearn for a sound that is missing.

The episode hovers between the past and the present of the poem. Achille is reintroduced to the tribe's collective memory. The tribe 'muttered about a future Achille already knew' and about 'who the serpent god conducted miles off his course for some blasphemous offence and how he would pay for it / by forgetting his parents, his tribe and his own spirit / for an albino god'. The barnacled cannons of wrecked slaving galleons of the Middle Passage (across the Atlantic from Africa), with their sprouting anemones, are likened to Philoctete's skin; the rusted anchors are like crossbows, still able to wound. In a reversal of Homeric identities, to his ancestor it is Achille who is the ghost – 'Are you smoke from a fire that never burned', for of course in the African context he never existed.

The final sequence tells why. 'The raid was profitable.' 'The doors were like open graves' (book 3.XXVII.I p. 145). Achille watches as the chained men are taken away. He foresees their future, with the tinkling of the coins that will be exchanged for them matching that of the irons which will chain them. Arrow shafts lie in the dust. His rage re-enacts the frenzied hatred of Achilles in *Iliad* 21 after Hector has killed Patroclus. He rushes to rescue the men but is caught by the heel in 'a cord of thorned vine'.

Finally, the Middle Passage is equated with an underworld of its own, a purgatory of suffering:

> We were the colour of shadows when we came down
> with tinkling leg-irons to join the chains of the sea,
> for the silver coins multiplying on the sold horizon,
>
> and these shadows are reprinted now on the white sand
> of antipodal coasts, your ashen ancestors
> from the Bight of Benin, from the margin of Guinea
> *Omeros* book 3.XXVIII.I p. 149

> There was an enforced change in their sense of identity –
> each man was a nation
> in himself, without mother, father, brother
> *Omeros* book 3.XXVIII.I p. 150

Walcott tells how, united only in suffering, they wept for practical things and only later, with growing realisation of loss, for their gods and their language. 'But they crossed, they survived. There is the epical splendour' (*Omeros* book 3.XXVIII.I p. 149).

This is surely a new kind of epic, a poem which identifies and uses fragments or sherds from ancient epic, drawing in Greek and Roman resonances within the formal frameworks and refiguring them to create a plural consciousness which acknowledges the force of the past but recognises that revisiting the past, whether Greek, Roman or African is, on its own, not enough. The *katabasis* in *Omeros* rams home in the prow of Achille's canoe another awful truth, that 'roots' cannot be totally recaptured or relived. Yet at the same time as he shows this, Walcott's poem also recognises that neither the historical nor the literary past is obliterated. For Walcott 'the sea sighs with the drowned from the Middle Passage'.[8]

The quasi-*katabasis* in *Omeros* works in partnership with the web of imagery and allusions associated with Philoctete to subvert two assumptions. The first is that the poet's epic voice is simply derivative or is unproblematically influenced by ancient epic. The second assumption is that Walcott's exploration of the history and causes of Philoctete's wound entails creating a Caribbean identity which is merely that of victims of slavery and exploitation. The *katabasis* recognises the past but in imagining it reveals its disjunction from the present. Nostalgia for an identity delineated only by African roots is rejected. The implications of this refiguration are twofold. First, the conclusions are controversial, signalling an emergence of what might be described as a post-post-colonial literary and cultural consciousness. Secondly, the poetic techniques through which this new consciousness is achieved carry with them an explicit rejection of dependence on an unexamined 'classical heritage'.

Some critics have used the concept of *mimicry* (whether of ancient epic or of western literature in general), as an accusation of literary and ideological dependency which suggests that the poet has failed to renounce the language and literature of former colonial powers. Greek and Roman literature has frequently been included in the category of colonial literature, both because of its appropriation by western imperial powers as part of their systems of education and values, and because of the force exercised by the literature and ideas of the Graeco-Roman world on subsequent cultures in Europe and North America.[9] In the context of the translation issues being discussed in this book the use of the word mimicry in post-colonial situations adds a political dimension to the cluster of stylistic and cultural associations referred to in the debates about translational relationships discussed in Chapter 1.

6. Walcott's Philoctete: Imaging the Post-Colonial Condition

Walcott himself discussed the concept in an early article 'The Caribbean: culture or mimicry', written when he was Director of the Trinidad Theatre Company in Port of Spain.[10] He considered the extent to which powerlessness left the ex-colonial world no alternative but to imitate the political systems of the major powers and also their art, language and philosophy. Against this tendency he ranged alternatives, including revolutionary rejection of colonising cultures or various kinds of assimilation. All these processes, he argued, lead eventually to metamorphosis, because to reflect, mirror or mimic other cultures, while it may be a starting point, ultimately involves despair and failure ('we cannot return to what we have never been'); 'the New World originated in hypocrisy and genocide, so it is not a question for us, of returning to an Eden or creating Utopia'. As an example of metamorphosis, he examines Carnival – 'This is a mass art form which came out of nothing, which emerged from the sanctions imposed on it. The banning of African drumming led to the discovery of the garbage can cover as a potential musical instrument whose subtlety of range, transferred to an empty oil drum, increases yearly, and the calypso itself emerged from a sense of mimicry ... the calypso supersedes its ancient ritual forms in group cleansing. From the viewpoint of history, these forms originated in imitation if you want, and ended in invention.'[11]

Walcott has addressed these issues from two standpoints. First, he has acknowledged the impact of colonisation and its aftermath, including the influence of radical writers such as Fanon and Césaire whom he regards as energisers of both Caribbean and American culture. Many critics and interpreters of post-colonial literature have followed or adapted Fanon's formulations of the three-stage development of the writings of colonised peoples (i.e. unqualified assimilation; exoticism; creators of a revolutionary or national literature), and increasingly there has been an appreciation of the relationship between stages of literary development and stages of the development of national or regional consciousness and cultural identity, involving assertion of difference from the dominant imperial culture.[12]

Secondly, however, Walcott has given these propositions a radical twist by emphasising that the model for post-colonial literatures is intercultural. This opens the way to polyphony and interaction rather than retaining a simple opposition of colonisers and colonised. Walcott is advocating mixing and hybridity rather than separatism. Thirdly, and perhaps most subversively of all, he has emphasised that the metamorphosis embraces not only the culture of the colonisers but also the previous 'history' and tradition of the colonised, including aspects of their identity which have an existence in 'memory' but are not fully recoverable.

This realisation is contained in but not limited by Walcott's perception of the fractured relationship which Caribbean peoples have with the African past, a relationship which was broken not only by the diaspora brought about by slavery and the Middle Passage but also by subsequent racial and cultural hybridity. 'The claim which we put forward as Africans now is not our inheritance, but a bequest, like that of other races, a bill for the condition of your arrival as slaves. Our own ancestors shared that complicity and there is no one left on whom we can exact revenge' (Walcott, 1974, p. 10).

So for Walcott, 'mimicry' is actually part of a process of beginning anew, part of 'the painful, new, laborious uttering that comes out of belief not out of doubt. Creativity (as Walcott emphasises in *The Muse of History*), cannot come out of revenge. The quasi-*katabasis* in *Omeros* draws on Homer, Vergil, Dante and African tradition but mimics none of them. Nostalgia is replaced by refiguration. *Omeros* embraces the results of Walcott's mature reflections on assimilation, mimicry and revolution in literature and culture and displays a corresponding confidence in inventiveness derived from that 'cunning metamorphosis' developed in his earlier work and thought. The translational techniques developed in the poem – names, metaphors, allusions and adaptation of literary icons, conventions and episodes – are used to shape and fire this refiguration. Taken together they suggest a new kind of translational equivalence, that of the processes and dynamics involved in transplanting classical referents into a new cultural context and their nurturing and transfiguration into a new literary enterprise.

All this is not so far from the sources in Homer, Sophocles and Vergil as it may seem. In their different ways the works of all these poets grew from engagement with mythological tradition, historical memory and more recent ideological and cultural contexts. Homer is, of course, a special case partly because of the oral tradition which generated the *Iliad* and the *Odyssey* and 'Homeric' characteristics of style. With

Homer, perhaps, the 'equivalence' is in some respects at its most resonant. Homeric epic emerged from the interaction of sea-borne cultures in which traces of stories, legends and myths, sometimes overlapping, were crafted together and given new form and direction in a Greek context.[13] This kind of cultural metamorphosis and invention finds a modern equivalence in Walcott's new epic, an epic which in order to create the new has taken an interventionist stance towards the ancient sources, texts and images and also towards newer assumptions about Caribbean culture and its relationship to African and to European traditions.

7

Translating Genres (i)

The sea speaks the same language around the world's shores.
Walcott, *The Odyssey: A Stage Version*[1]

An underlying theme in some of the earlier chapters has been the way writers have experimented in using genres different from that of the original to represent equivalence or to transplant images in ways that enable new work to grow. Recent work in both poetry and theatre has involved 'genre cross-over', particularly from epic to lyric (in the poems of Michael Longley) and to dramatic monologue (Carol Ann Duffy), from epic to stage drama (in the work of Peter Oswald, Botho Strauss and Derek Walcott on the *Odyssey*), from poem to physical theatre (Ted Hughes, *Tales from Ovid*, staged by the Royal Shakespeare Company) and from drama to film poem (or verse film) in Tony Harrison's *Prometheus*. This last crossover raises the further question of the impact of twentieth-century technology on translational possibilities, an aspect highlighted in the experiments with video and multi-media techniques, such as the Theatre Cryptic's *Electra* (Sophocles) 1999 and the Royal National Theatre version of Ted Hughes' translation of *The Oresteia*, 1999.

In this chapter, I shall begin by focussing on two recent stage versions of Homer's *Odyssey* by Oswald and Walcott in order to explore the relationship between narrative and direct speech in epic poetry and staged drama and to consider the cultural contexts which shaped the creation and reception of the performances. In the next chapter I shall turn to the relationship between film and the interventionist translation techniques used by Harrison in his version of *Prometheus*.

The first thing to be said is that epic poetry and tragic drama in Greece were in any case closely related genres. Tragedy was in a constantly revisionist relationship with the myths that were part of Homer and the Epic Cycle. Thus tragedy drew on the language, imagery, rhetoric and formal characteristics of oral poetry and refigured them in a different cultural context.[2] In one sense the Greek dramatists had a translational relationship with the Homeric poems as well as with the broader field of myth within which Homer worked. Yet of course staging also involves the creation of framing devices which are very different from those of epic poetry (even if the poem is communicated or performed orally). Epic poetry has a narrator through whom other voices are articulated and by whom the listeners' experience is shaped. Sometimes these may be narrators within the narrative.[3] In drama that explicit narrative frame is hidden behind the characters in the play and the action on stage. A different kind of 'reality' is created, that of the immediate world of the stage in which people move and gesture and interact as well as speak and in which they rarely address the audience directly. The audience are spectators, and the range of imaginative responses and ranges of meaning can be directed and limited by what is represented on the stage and how it is represented. Radio drama does sometimes give scope for the linking narrative voice, for example Timberlake Wertenbaker's *Deianeira* (BBC Radio 3, December 1999) which included a narrative within a narrative to explain the relationship between the authors, the storyteller and the play. Nevertheless, in general a staged performance which operates as visual spectacle rather than aural experience has to develop narrative techniques which can be integrated into the staging.

The stage versions of the *Odyssey* created by Oswald and by Walcott adopted very different approaches to this issue, and in each case the strategies chosen not only shaped the actual performance but represented a different perspective on Homer's poem.

Peter Oswald's verse translation/stage adaptation of Homer's *Odyssey* was staged by the Gate Theatre Company in 1999 and toured nationally in the UK, directed by Martin Wylde (published text Peter Oswald, *Odysseus*). Neither Oswald nor Wylde is a Greek scholar and they consulted 'several different translations some literal, some not' and eventually agreed to base the adaptation on Richmond Lattimore's translation.[4] The programme notes proclaimed Homer's story 'the most famous life journey in western culture' and this set the tone for the adaptation of the material. The version was concerned only with Odysseus' return to Ithaca, with the emphasis on the soul-searching that accompanied his re-integration, the 'voyage of self discovery that is Homer's true subject'. For Wylde 'the power of the sea and the fantastic journey was a metaphor for the psychological journey Odysseus undergoes on his return ... In rehearsals we looked a great deal at post traumatic stress disorder; how this expresses itself and can be come to terms with'.

At the beginning of the production, Odysseus lay as if dead on the foreshore. The set was bounded by the broken wall of a house with Odysseus' great bow set at the side. There were seats for the players, who remained on stage all the time, stepping forward onto a low white raised platform when participating in the action. Members of the cast also functioned as a kind of Chorus (wearing half-masks) and their role was crucial in translating the impact of the narrative voice in epic onto the stage and in representing aspects of Odysseus' dreadful voyage, including the episodes which tested his resolution and ingenuity. His recollections of the sufferings of his companions were represented by the Chorus who also functioned as occasional commentators on the inter-relationship of the action and imagery, for instance when Odysseus and Penelope encountered one another:

> Now a sea whispers to a sea
> And just a streak of land between.
> Oswald, *Odysseus* scene 6 p. 41

The use in adapted form of Greek dramatic conventions was integral to this emphasis on the mind of Odysseus. The Chorus was given a corporate identity by the use of translucent half-masks with gold painted inside. The actor's faces could be glimpsed underneath. Identified by the masks, the actors were linked together while still retaining individuality. Their role on stage was 'expressionistic; they were voices inside Odysseus' head; the dead from his past that haunted him' (Wylde). The actors who remained present on the stage outside the main playing space also had a role. A second Chorus was formed by the actors sitting round the stage and watching the scenes in which they were not directly involved. This Chorus was one of observers, of 'the people' watching. Although this Chorus did not speak it may have had closer resemblance to a 'Greek' chorus (Wylde).

Wylde has also emphasised the relationship between the staging and design of the play and the fact that it was a touring production aimed at a wide audience. 'The set needed to be simple, light and able to be set up or taken down by two people in a couple of hours ... the simplicity required of the set led Roger Butlin, the designer, and myself to develop a fairly abstract space that could be defined by light and the words. We would probably have followed this course regardless of the space and funds available. Also, the touring nature [of the production] encouraged us to keep the actors on stage for the entire play to simplify entrances and exits although again we would probably have done this for artistic reasons. The space did limit how much movement was feasible in the production.'

The role of the Chorus enabled the staging to recreate something of the impact of the complex time sequence in Homer's epic, especially the flash-backs, narrative loops and echoes of past experiences. However, the Chorus could not provide equivalence for Homer's foreshadowing techniques and it was left to Athena to anticipate the deaths of the suitors:

> It is my wish that with the blood
> And entrails of ungracious men
> Your palace shall be spattered soon.
> > Scene 3 p. 18

A variety of theatrical techniques was used to create the scenes with the suitors and Odysseus' stringing of the bow. The audience's sense of involvement was provoked when they were addressed by Antinoos as if they were suitors and when Odysseus pointed the bow as if to shoot. Odysseus' reasserted heroic status was accompanied by percussion, a shout of 'Achilles', sudden darkness and then the entry of Telemachos to report the death of the suitors. This made the final scene of delayed recognition between Penelope and Odysseus rather an anti-climax. Nevertheless the low-key conversation brought out the ironies of the double standards of epic morality. Odysseus contrasted Penelope with Helen and Clytemnestra. She questioned him about his relationship with Circe and Calypso, drawing perhaps on Homer *Odyssey* 23.219-24. This passage (possibly a later addition) implies that the love between Helen and the foreigner Paris was pursued in ignorance about the outcome. The simple but effective lighting design (which had shifted to mauve at points of heightened psychological tension) then softened, and the audience was reassured by a happy ending.

The production's urgent and verbally packed translation sometimes used strong rhythmic rhyme patterns ('and something caught my eye / Far down the smoky alley of the sky': scene 7 p. 49) and at other points suggestive and delicate half-rhymes. The imaginative adaptation of Greek dramatic conventions overcame some of the problems of staging epic storytelling. A late twentieth-century audience attuned to exploration of psychological trauma and to the ironies of gendered double standards were also drawn into something of the flavour of the epic:

> I saw Achilles, glory of the world
> Burned on a big pyre, watched his grey smoke age
> The moon, that maiden, and I turned to stare
> At Troy unsightly as the sun fell speared
>
> Scene 7 p. 48

It was certainly theatrically and aesthetically justified to concentrate on the Ithacan section of Homer's poem, but this was a sanitised homecoming. Penelope had no loom and had developed no *kleos* of her own, so the impact of her banishment to the upper room as a contrast to her previous foreground role in Homer's poem was largely absent.

Above all, there were no maids to be hung, no blood to be cleansed, no pollution requiring the house to be fumigated and therefore no deep ambiguities in the healing of Odysseus' mind and in his re-establishment as master of the household.

> ... And so I cast off No One
> And watch him sink into the deepening
> Of the sea's eye.
>
> Scene 9 p. 61

The question remained whether it was possible in crossing genres from epic to stage to create a version which was both of the late twentieth century and yet engaged with the Homeric issues, a version in which equivalence also embraces recognition of difference. That this version did not achieve this was governed partly by its method of translating narrative techniques to the stage, partly by the limited

117

physicality of the acting styles and, perhaps, partly by the emphasis on translating those parts of the Homeric experience with which modern audiences could empathise. There is a useful distinction to be made between two main types of audience involvement, the authorial and the narrative.[5] The authorial audience is sophisticated and can respond to metatheatrical or contemporary allusion and to the nuances of the relationship between the source text and its modern refiguration, whereas the narrative audience temporarily consents to believe a world of fiction, responding to the story as it unfolds. The Oswald/Wylde *Odyssey* did not seek to challenge members of the audience to be able to do *both* of these things, but as compensation it gained aesthetically and theatrically from its coherent integration of poetry, design and narrative substitutes.

In contrast Derek Walcott's *The Odyssey: A Stage Version*, directed by Gregory Doran (1992), did manage to provoke both engagement and metatheatrical reflection. Like the Oswald/Wylde version, its shape and ethos were initially set by the way it engaged with the issue of the narrators; unlike Oswald/Wylde, the Walcott/Doran version was ebullient and sometimes undisciplined.

Walcott's play opens with the figure of the blind blues singer Billy Blue:

> Gone sing 'bout that man because his stories please us,
> Who saw trials and tempests for ten years after Troy
>
> I'm Blind Billy Blue, my main man's sea-smart Odysseus,
> Who the God of the Sea drove crazy and tried to destroy.
>
> Andra moi ennepe mousa polutropon hos mala polla ...
> The shuttle of the sea moves back and forth on this line,
>
> All night like the surf, she shuttles and doesn't fall
> Asleep, then her rosy fingers at dawn unstitch the design.
> Act I, Prologue p. 1

Within a cultural framework enlarged to contain the seas to the New World, beyond Greece and Troy, the themes and images are those of Homer: many-sided Odysseus, the daily deferral of arrival and certainty. The image of Penelope's loom is transposed to comprehend the movement of the sea and the reversal of night and day. (In the 1992 rehearsal text, this Prologue to Act I contained the stage direction 'silhouette of Penelope weaving by torchlight'). Just as the Homeric bard Demodocus sang the adventures of heroes within the *Odyssey*, so Billy Blue is the emblem of the relationship between diaspora and artistic invention. In the second act Demodocus explicitly makes the point that the story of Odysseus moves everywhere with the sea. 'The sea speaks the same language round the world's shores' (II.IV.122). The 'sameness' of this language is, in fact, constituted by diversity and by recognition that this involves a dynamic interplay of cultures. The notion of commonality in language and cultural referents of course brings its own problems. The idea of overlap between otherwise differentiated circles of experience may, in concentrating on what is held in common, exclude the dynamics generated by diverse contributions from the borders and thus reduce rather than enlarge consciousness. Walcott's response to this 'problem' is to centralise the margins, and one important aspect of this is his dramatisation of the role of Billy Blue. In this way, Walcott simultaneously improvises on the theme of travelling bards in ancient Greece and gives a shaping voice to twentieth-century black consciousness.

Blues music carries the memory of the past (including slavery and diaspora), but the virtuosity of the Blues is a phenomenon of contemporary culture, creating its own language and resonances and engaging a new community of listeners. So in one sense translation of the *Odyssey* from epic to staged drama also involves another kind of genre cross-over, that of the rhythms and modulations of the Blues. Walcott has stated that his aim was to introduce 'the most emblematic figure we have in the twentieth century ... someone who contains a history of the race ... someone who sings ballads, the preserver of the cultural memory'.[6]

Other aspects of the play's production also grew from this kind of translational practice. The figure of Eurykleia, Odysseus' old nurse and the first to recognise him on his return to Ithaca, is also developed by both aural and oral memories. The speech rhythms and dramatic impact of her role originate at least in part from Caribbean culture and draw on the resonance of the ante-bellum plantation culture of the southern states of the USA. It is she who is represented as 'the cradle', both figuratively in terms of memory, like Billy Blue, and literally: as Telemachus says, 'to me and my father you have been slave and nurse' (I.II.9).

This theme plays a key role in the dramatic reversal at the climax of the play and is made to permeate the play through the guiding voice and idiom of the Homeric bard figure Billy Blue and also by the double consciousness created in the audience by the interplay of language and staging. This had the effect of communicating *both* the oral history of the oppression of their race *and* that they were the source of insights which were a necessary part of the narrative and dramatic structure of the play.[7] The delivery of narrative authority and insight through the translational force of music, gesture, costume, setting and acting styles (for instance in the carnival-style enactment of the Calypso episode) actually resulted in what the critic Homi Bhabha has described as a 'translational culture'. He used the term to indicate a new site of cultural production in which previously marginalised voices are heard and through which perspectives are transformed.[8]

The strategies of translation themselves led to a new and challenging reversal at the end of the play. This occurs in the sequence which I shall call Penelope's Wrath. In Homer, wrath is a masculine quality. In the *Iliad*, for instance, the wrath of Achilles is a motivating force for the action when the male heroes on the beach before Troy quarrel about reputation, power and control. In Homer's *Odyssey* Penelope does not display wrath. On the contrary, she is patient. The epithets applied to her are 'shining' and 'virtuous'. Nevertheless it is an innovative feature of Homer's treatment of the myth that she is associated with the idea of *kleos* (lasting glory and fame) which is an attribute of heroes. Some critics dispute whether *kleos* is attributed directly to Penelope in Homer's poem or whether she and Odysseus share in a joint *kleos* (as Penelope implies at *Odyssey* 18.255 and 19.128). If the former, this is unique for a woman in Greek literature. If the latter, the sharing of *kleos* is nevertheless significant, a part of the like-mindedness which is a feature of the poem.[9] Aspiring to or possessing *kleos* implies that someone has gained confidence in their identity and that this is recognised by current and future communities as a model.

Homer's Penelope is, clearly, not a mouse. However, the nearest she is permitted to come to wrath is a feeling of indignation, a word used by Hanna Roisman.[10] In her discussion of the issue Roisman explored what it was *Homerically* plausible for Penelope to be indignant about – that Odysseus did not immediately reveal himself and left her in continuing anxiety about the return of an impostor who might be using evil tricks to deceive her (23.216-17). According to Roisman, by her coolness and delaying of recognition Penelope in effect exerts her power to delay Odysseus' resumption of his mastery of the household. This caution underlies Penelope's response to the nurse's rejoicing over the death of the suitors (23.58-9):

> Circumspect Penelope said to her in answer:
> Dear nurse, do not yet laugh aloud in triumph.

Penelope at this point is withholding her approval. However, this is because of the manner of Odysseus' return and not because she disapproves of the slaughter of the suitors (which she regards as an act expressing divine retribution, 23.83-4). Indeed, in Homer it is Odysseus who shows restraint after the slaughter and insists on religious purification (22.480).

In Walcott's *Stage Version* Penelope is constructed as a woman of strength, who does possess *kleos* and does express wrath. Her wrath is derived both from the causes of her 'indignation' in Homer and from causes on which Homer is silent. These Homeric silences are activated by the demands of modern performance and transformed by the translational techniques involved in Walcott's transplantation of the story across cultures. In Walcott's version, Odysseus sees the suitors as warriors, emblematic of the effects of the war:

> Troy's mulch. Troy's rain! Wounds. Festering diseases!
>
> II.VI.151

and he slaughters them ('wrestling the god for his mind' as Eumaeus puts it). Penelope's reaction is that 'This cunning beggar is the smartest of suitors' (II.VI.153). This is an echo of Homer's justification for her indignation. But this is not all. She also reacts strongly against the actual killing:

> You had to wade this deep in blood?
>
> II.VI.153

121

In Homer, Odysseus' *aristeia* is relatively unproblematic. This is also true of Oswald's version, but not of Walcott's. When Odysseus justifies his actions as necessary to reclaim his house, Penelope is outraged

> What house? You mean this abattoir?
>   II.VI.153

In a black parody of the home and hearth image, Odysseus replies that 'It's you I killed for' but Penelope does not fall into his arms – 'It's for this I kept my thighs crossed for twenty years?' In a striking inversion of the Telemachus theme, which in Homer involves Telemachus seeking not only to find his father but to emulate him, Walcott's Penelope accuses Odysseus of being an obscene example to his son, leading him towards a second Troy (II.VI.154). The whole agenda for negotiation is changed, and in the next sequence in the scene Penelope's wrath ensures that the maidservant Melantho is not hanged. In Homer's *Odyssey* the hanging of the serving women, who are denounced by the nurse Eurykleia, is carried out by Telemachus in punishment for their (perhaps enforced) relationship with the suitors (22.457-72). He rigs up a ship's cable and fastens them to it 'so their heads were all in a line and each had her neck caught fast in a noose so that their death would be most pitiful'. Like Walcott's Melantho, the serving women in Homer are said to be guilty of 'insolence'. The word used in Homer means 'shamelessness' and is one which is also applied to inanimate objects. The Homeric image of the hanging has attracted the attention of modern poets, for instance in Peter Reading's 'Homeric' (*Collected Poems 2*, Bloodaxe Books 1996) and Michael Longley's 'The Butchers' (*Gorse Fires*, Secker and Warburg 1991). Both poets follow the Homeric version closely.

The image also has wider literary resonances, notably in Margaret Atwood's *The Handmaid's Tale* (Virago 1987). The novel takes up a number of classical models in its portrayal of the sexual, economic and political oppression of women in a contemporary fundamentalist totalitarian state. In Atwood's book, women are known by the names of their masters – Offred and so on – following the practice in ancient Greece of referring to women as the wife of X or the daughter of Y. Such a loss of personal identity also has a role in *The Handmaid's Tale*. The disappeared become Unwomen, Unbabies. In Atwood's novel the procedures in a Salvaging follow the model in Homer's *Odyssey*. A Salvaging is a rope ceremony in which delinquent women are hung on a line. The killings are supervised by women, like Eurykleia, who are called the Aunts: 'There were many women willing to serve as aunts, either because of a genuine belief in what they called "traditional values" or for the benefits they might therefore acquire' (p. 320). Atwood's novel reveals how the Homeric hanging of abused serving women attained the status of a *topos* in twentieth-century feminist consciousness. Walcott's Penelope not only refuses complicity in this abuse, she prevents it.

However, it would be a mistake to read the incident merely in terms of gender. It is not, after all, that Walcott is sympathetic to feminism. Indeed, he has expressly denied that the serving maid is spared for that reason – 'it's not because of feminism and all that stuff'.[11] Walcott is also on record as saying that conformity to expectation derived from race and gender stereotypes and class engagement is inhibiting to writers and that 'insiderism' is fatal to their development.[12]

Nevertheless, Walcott acknowledged of his reversal of Homer at this point in the play: 'it is a radical change ... I wanted somebody who was in a rage. I don't want to make a sort of marble statue.' It is also the case that Walcott acknowledged that he felt uncomfortable about the staged killing of the serving maid before a twentieth-century audience, in other words because of the emotions, values and dramatic coherence of the play and the audience's response to its interventionist and transformative power. He firmly rejected the possibility of a feminist discourse (which might after all have required Penelope to reject Odysseus), but the play recognises that the renegotiation of the relationship between Penelope and Odysseus gives her some say in the process of her redomestication.

Crucial to this is the fact that Walcott's *Odyssey* is poetry in performance. Enacting the hanging would have had a performative impact far in excess of a recitation. As he said in an interview in 1992, 'You could just say "and he hanged all the women". You know, recite that.' Walcott was equally concerned about the image of his hero: 'It was very difficult to have any sympathy for someone who, no matter what he went through, at the end could give an order to hang all the maids in the house.' So it seems that there are a number of interwoven rationales for Walcott's reversal of Homer. First, the aesthetic dynamic means that he wants Penelope to show her anger and to act, not to be regarded as a marble statue (a pervasive image in the play, referring both to Penelope and to ancient culture as material and inactive objects). Secondly, although Walcott rejects feminist perspectives, the language and action of the play in fact identify the serving maid with an exploited slave class. In the Royal Shakespeare Company production (The Other Place, Stratford-upon-Avon, 1992) she was played by a black actress, doubled with Nausicaa, and the text made the connection explicit. Melantho's 'shameless' behaviour was presented as a corruption of the princess's innocence. Thirdly, performance actively engages the audience in the construction of meaning. This requires some coherence in the way the speech and action of the play are presented. The audience can then relate these to conventions and values external to the world of the play. Walcott's version makes extensive use of such authentication – in the persona of the Blues singer; in the representation of the Cyclops as a totalitarian monster; he can do no less in terms of Penelope. This kind of interdependence between language and action in a play and its 'real' application has been identified by critics as an example of a politics of plausibility.[13]

Walcott's *Odyssey* is presented to the audience not as an attempt at reproduction or even imitation but as a kind of extended simile, and in a curious way this has made the dynamic patterns of the play more equivalent to those in the Greek than an 'authentic' or archaeological reproduction would be. For in Homer Penelope, too, has in the end to be made to conform to audience expectations. In that case the expectations were those of the social conservatism applying at that time, whether derived from the masculinist ideals of the heroic past represented in the poems or from the values of the society which heard the recitations, a society allied with the peasant values documented by Hesiod in *Works and Days*. In either case, Homer's radicalism could go only so far. The politics of plausibility required that Penelope could not challenge the male dominated values of the *oikos*, or household. And so despite her embryonic *kleos* and her status as an exception to the developing misogyny of Greek literature, she is repositioned back in the upper chamber. In Homer's *Odyssey* 23.365 her role is to 'sit still, looking at no one and do not ask any questions'. She disappears from the action, becoming the cultural equivalent of what Walcott describes as a museum piece or marble statue. In Walcott's *Odyssey*, however,

Penelope cannot aesthetically or politically remain a statue. The translational techniques involved in crossing from epic to drama and from *koine* Mediterranean culture to Atlantic/Caribbean have created a new cultural site with norms which have to be observed, just as Homer (or his co-practitioners) had to. The task of the cultural historian has been described as 'to recover contexts or horizons of expectation'.[14] In the case of Penelope's Wrath the expectations of ancient and modern audiences collide. In that sense the politics of plausibility are a decisive factor in the reversals which take place at the end of Homer's epic and Walcott's *Stage Version*. Walcott's shifting of translational norms has as one of its effects a redirection of the attention of the 'authorial' audience back to the political dynamics of Homer's epic.

8

Translating Genres (ii)

How can Olympus stay intact
if *poetry* comes to *Pontefract*?
(Voice of Hermes) Tony Harrison,
Prometheus (1998) p. 23

The dynamic relationship between cultural icon and intervention is even more central to Tony Harrison's verse film *Prometheus* than to Walcott's revitalisation of the images of statues and vases in *The Odyssey: A Stage Version*. In Harrison's verse-film words and images work together. The film begins in a Yorkshire mining village as the pit is about to be closed down. The miner's son is learning about Prometheus at school. ('He stole fire from t'gods and gave it to men down here. So now there's coal and all that. He ended up chained to a rock for thirty thousand years and a bloody great eagle came and ate his liver every day, as a punishment for stealing fire' (p. 9). The boy lights the fire at home and inadvertently destroys a collection of press cuttings about the Miner's Strike of 1984. His father is so enraged that he hurls into the fire both the boy's schoolbook and a carving of a miner in pit gear in a Prometheus-like pose. The themes of fire, poetry, history and the potential of technology for good and evil frame the film. The creation of the golden statue of Prometheus from the remains of the redundant miners who are thrown into a furnace, its journey through polluted Europe on a lorry and its eventual meltdown in the final conflagration provide the critical spine of the narrative within the film, and at each stage of its creation and journey the statue throws out sparks which illuminate the interface between the Greek myth and the condition of twentieth-century Europe.

There are two features of the history of the Prometheus image and its role in intervention and in transforming cultural norms which are particularly significant here. The first is the malleability of the myth.

The persistence of the main characteristics of the figure of Prometheus contrasts with its flexibility for construction in a range of media and genres. As a figure, Prometheus has historically been an icon for defiance and humanistic struggle, represented as a victim or appropriated for 'causes' rather than being a vehicle for psychological analysis or an example of metamorphosis. The main points about Prometheus in the treatment of the ancient myth in the fifth-century tragedy attributed to Aeschylus are that he defies Zeus, brings fire to men, and subsequently remains intransigent in the face of threats from Zeus. This suggests that Prometheus as a model is susceptible to appropriation by interventionists.

Thus the figure of Prometheus, precisely because of the precision of its characteristics, can serve as an agent for linking together the causes and issues for which it is appropriated. In the trilogy attributed to Aeschylus, only one play of which has survived, the myth of Prometheus is thought to have been developed in three sequences: Prometheus the Creator or Firebringer; the extant play *Prometheus Bound* (or *in Chains*); and Prometheus Unbound or Freed by Herakles. These three broad strands seem to have shaped subsequent representations of Prometheus in various media, and this has continued across the arts in the twentieth century.[1] The three strands come together in the Prometheus trilogy, three gilded bronze sculpture sketches by Paul Manship (1950) with casts in the Minnesota Museum of Art. Manship also has a Prometheus (with torch) as a gilded bronze fountain figure at the Rockefeller Centre, New York. Kokoschka's *The Prometheus Saga* is a triptych ceiling painting (1950, private collection, London) which features 'Prometheus Bound'. The other panels are 'Apocalypse' (including Apollo turning away and Aeneas rescuing Anchises) and 'Hades and Persephone' (with Persephone emerging from the Underworld as a messenger of Spring). The associations testify to the variety of possibilities in which the situation of Prometheus, condemned by Zeus to be chained to a rock in perpetuity with his liver gnawed away by eagles, might imaginatively and symbolically be resolved.

In dance, Ninette de Valois created the choreography and scenario for a ballet *Prometheus*, using music by Beethoven. This was first performed in 1936 at Sadler's Wells. In 1970 Frederick Ashton was the creator of the choreography and scenario of *Die Geschöpfe des*

8. Translating Genres (ii)

Prometheus (*The Creatures of Prometheus*) with music by John Lanch-bery (after Beethoven), first performed in Bonn. These examples demonstrate the versatility and plasticity of the myth across a range of media and also point to the way in which transmission (including subject matter, style and content) involves various kinds of intra-textual and inter-textual relationships.

In terms of ideas, twentieth-century approaches have been deeply conscious of the late eighteenth- and early nineteenth-century associa-tion between Prometheus and the Romantic movement. In literature the major figures are Goethe (1773) and Schlegel (1797) in German, and in English Percy Bysshe Shelley, whose *Prometheus Unbound* was published in London in 1820. Mary Shelley called her work *Franken-stein or The Modern Prometheus* (1818), thus pointing to the uneasy relationship between creativity and the torment of a flawed figure. Allusions to other aspects of the myth's potential are widespread, especially in Byron, who in his poem *Prometheus* (1816) explored endurance of the suffering which resulted from opposition to the gods. Byron also used the Prometheus image as a yardstick for comparison with the exile of Napoleon (*Ode to Napoleon Bonaparte 1814*, stanza 16).

More humanistically, Robert Browning addressed Prometheus' en-lightenment of human beings in his dramatic monologue 'With Bernard de Mandeville' (stanzas 10-11) in *Parleyings with certain people of importance in their day* (1887). Towards the end of the nineteenth century, Gerard Manley Hopkins translated lines 88-100 and 114-127 of the Greek as 'Promêtheus Desmotês'. The influence of the play on Hopkins is evident from his Notebooks and Letters, especially in respect of his development of new rhythmic forms in English. Critics have frequently discussed the relationship between Hopkins' close reading and translation of Greek texts and his later innovative work.[2]

Most importantly in the nineteenth century, the *Prometheus Bound* became important as a play for translation, and this defines the second important strand of influence of the Prometheus figure, its role as a catalyst for the development of further work. I discussed in Chapter 2 some of the ways in which nineteenth-century translators used their translation activity as a springboard for further radical and creative work, and translating *Prometheus* seems to have played a notable role

129

in this. Not only was translating the play a rite of passage for women translators, it seems also to have inspired them in interventionist directions and to have shaped their response to the issues of obligation, community, freedom, tyranny and oppression of women, all of which were raised by the play.

The role of the *Prometheus Bound* as a catalyst for cultural debate and artistic innovation intensified in the twentieth century. In the 1920s the Greek poet Angelos Sikelianos and his American wife Eva Palmer developed the Delphic Idea. They wished to establish at the omphalos (navel of the earth at Delphi) a university based on a spiritual and communal ideal of world peace, and in 1927 a Festival was held at which tragedy was performed, together with athletics and folk dancing. Part of the performance of the Prometheus (in Chains, in the translation by I. Gryparis) has been preserved on film. One of the aims was to recreate ancient Greek performance, and the costumes and movements of the Chorus were derived from images on Greek vase paintings, although it has also been suggested that Palmer's early training by Isadora Duncan gave the choreography a more modern character.[3] As a result of the 1927 performance and another festival in 1930 at which the play was again revived, the staging of ancient drama became a subject of study and debate, not only in terms of the perceived need to perform in an authentic theatre but also in terms of the related questions of dance, choreography, setting and the aesthetic and symbolic use of theatrical space.[4]

The Delphi festivals attracted criticism from the radical press on the grounds that they were inaccessible to the public and encouraged cultural nostalgia, but they also stimulated debate about performance styles as well as initiating demand for the use of ancient Greek theatres for modern performances. All these issues have played an important role in Tony Harrison's versions of Greek drama. Staging in authentic theatres has been crucial for his *Oresteia* and *The Trackers of Oxyrhynchus*, and the question of the accessibility of the ideas and cultural implications especially so for his *Prometheus*. In sum, then, the history of refigurations of the Prometheus myth has been distinguished by the variety and inter-relationship of art forms used; by its role as a vehicle for radical voices and critique; its function as an energiser of and commentary on writers' other work; its influence as a catalyst for debate about cultural nostalgia and performance style. All these aspects, intensified by the genre cross-over to film, are evident in Harrison's *Prometheus*.[5]

The most important aspects of Harrison's choice of the verse-film as the genre for his *Prometheus* are probably the capability of film to give a voice and an image to the silenced and unrepresented, the potential of film as an interventionist medium for an audience different from that which would attend a Greek play, and his perception that the barbarities of the twentieth century require refigured forms of artistic expression. This last aim was set out in his earlier film-poem, *The Gaze of the Gorgon* (1992). The published text also contains a number of related poems, including the sequence 'Sonnets for August 1945' and 'Initial Illumination', a reflection on the Gulf War.

> The *barbitos*, the ancient lyre,
> since the Kaiser's day,
> is restrung with barbed wire
> Bard's hands bleed when they play
> the score that fits an era's scream,
> the blood, the suffering, the loss.
> The twentieth century theme
> is played on barbed wire *barbitos*.
> *The Gaze of the Gorgon*, p. 71

It is the conjunction of the moving images of film with poetry which, for Harrison, enables the poet to engage with the bloody twentieth-century themes through the framework of the Greek play. The play can provide this framework for three reasons: the cultural significance of the figure of the bound Prometheus; the analogy between the liberating technology associated with fire and the liberating power of poetry; and the mask (or distance) provided by the transplantation of the Greek conventions into a twentieth-century context. In his introduction to the published text, Harrison reflected that 'Most Greek tragedy shifts its timescale from immediate suffering to some long-term redemption through memorial ritual or social amelioration, or simply through the very play being performed ... Who calls from a remoter past than the bound Prometheus and yet who still manifests himself when history moves in directions where defiance and unfreedom cry for help?'[6]

Harrison also emphasises that if Aeschylus had been writing today he would have written a different play. However, while Harrison is clearly therefore not intending merely to reproduce Aeschylus' play in a more overtly twentieth-century sphere of application, he is nevertheless engaged in a task equivalent to that of Aeschylus: refiguring an ancient myth in the climate of the contemporary concerns of cultural politics, using a popular medium. In so doing, he is inviting the audience not just to transform its perspectives but to do so through a leap of the aesthetic imagination.

When Jonathan Miller (after directing Robert Lowell's *Prometheus* in the USA in 1967) said 'Classics are simply residues, maps left over from earlier cultures; they invite you to make some sort of imaginative movement', he was apparently referring to the relocation of an ancient play in time, place and language.[7] Harrison does all these things, but his demands on the 'imaginative movement' of the audience are even greater. The audience is also implicitly invited (and challenged) to reflect on the translational techniques involved in the interplay between language, moving images and the horizons of experience of the audience. These aspects of translation come together in the verse-film. In his preface to the text, Harrison discusses the underlying connection between verse, metrical poetry and film, suggesting that the 24 or 25 frames per second in the film have a 'prosodic motion' like the metrical beats in a verse line. Like poetry, the frames in the film succeed one another in a sequence with an inter-relationship which builds expectations and gratification. He considers that, just as in poetry 'the truthful word is also the right metrical word, the word with its truth and its sound placed on the most telling grid of the metric', so in cinematic construction experiencing and feeling the rhythm of the shots are like responding to truth in literature. And, he concludes, 'the two prosodies can be plaited, metrical beat and cinematic scansion'.

Various attempts have been made to classify the way in which Greek tragedy is represented on film. Probably the most influential was an approach by Jack J. Jorgens based on analysis of films of Shakespearean tragedies. The categories suggested by Jorgens are:

(i) theatrical mode – in which film is a recording device aiming to capture and preserve a theatrical performance.

(ii) realist mode, shifting the tragedy from a theatrical to a 'real'
    setting.
(iii) filmic mode, in which the creation of the film is itself a creation
    of the tragedy and the audience is complicit in a degree of artifice.

Harrison's *Prometheus* surely has aspects of both realist and filmic
modes. Yet in relating to both of these it also relates to a fourth
category, suggested by Kenneth MacKinnon.[10] This is the category of
meta-tragedy – that is, it includes an additional element of reflection
on the significance of the ancient tragedies to which the film relates.

Harrison's *Prometheus* uses moving images to locate the action in a
'real' environment. Initially this is the Yorkshire mining village emblematic of a community, socially devastated by pit closure in the
1980s but proudly marching behind the colliery band to the final day's
work. The theme of industrial decline is demonstrated Europe-wide
with shots of the suffering, exploitation and pollution resulting from
industrialisation under both capitalist and totalitarian regimes. The
mechanism linking the two modern environments is the 'film show' at
the derelict cinema in which the Old Man/Retired Miner/Prometheus
figure goes for a smoke to create nostalgia for the old times. At one
level, then, the potential for good and for bad of the technology
associated with the gift of fire is expressed in 'realistic' terms. However, the film within a film takes the work to metatheatrical mode, and
here Harrison's 'plaiting' of the rhythms of images and words combines
them to extend and transform the possibilities of meaning. The figure
of Hermes, speaking in semi-confidant role to the audience, tells how
Zeus has countered the liberating potential of Prometheus the firebringer (p. 33):

> And that play with its rebel views in
> needs spin-doctoring and defusing
> And that's where my slick skills come in.
> I'm employed to give Zeus spin
> And making statues is the way
> I've chosen to defuse that play.

The need for Zeus to find a way of depriving Prometheus of energy was
great, because

Poets have taught mankind to breach
the boundaries Zeus put round speech,
and the fire Prometheus stole
created man's poetic soul.

The boundaries which the tyrant Zeus 'put round speech' are burst in the play as the miners, imprisoned on a cattle truck, shed in their suffering their accustomed verbal conventions and begin to speak in verse, when as Harrison's phrase puts it 'poetry comes to Pontefract'.

However, this in itself presents a problem for the intratextual reflections of the film. If speaking in verse is a sign of human potential and the liberation of the mind and spirit, how is it that the boy's mother, Mam, the Io figure, has no voice at all? Once she has run through the remains of the mine buildings, she is shown at various points in a flight round devastated areas of Eastern Europe, her suffering relieved only by a few kind strangers (all women). In Aeschylus' play, Io is turned into a cow, pursued and tormented by a gadfly, because she has resisted Zeus' lust and offended his divine spouse. In Harrison's film, she is eventually cast into the cattle truck, with a Kafka-esque lack of explanation, and carted off to an abattoir, where in a devastating sequence of images she follows the route of the cattle to the stunning pen and is then hooked by the leg to be hung up on a meat hook. Like the cows in the slaughterhouse, she is by then black and white, but her colouring is achieved by the dirt and dust of chemicals and industrial pollution. The filmic impact is intense, but if the film represents a new kind of theatricality, a vehicle for submerged voices, then the inescapable message is that Mam/Io has no voice and no future, except perhaps in the survival of her son, seen at the end in his home village, watching as the old cinema burns. The silence of Mam/Io might be interpreted as an indictment of twentieth-century habits and art. Aeschylus gave Io major speeches, and in his play the suffering of Prometheus and of Io is structurally, narratively and metaphorically linked in that in both cases it stems from Zeus' misuse of power. Her silence in Harrison's film could also be a sign of the difficulty of engaging with gender abuse and political and social tyranny within a modern framework of references, because of audience resistance to such conflation. It could also follow from the power of the medium – film can give a 'voice' to the silenced without the necessity for them to speak.

8. Translating Genres (ii)

As well as representing the destruction of the miners and the suffering of Mam/Io, the film also relates the Prometheus myth to the sufferings of twentieth-century Europe. The long journey of the statue of Prometheus and the flight of Mam are used to mark in the narrative the bombing of Dresden, the Holocaust, and the disintegration of Eastern Europe and the Balkans. This merging of different strands of recent history within the framework of the myth has offended some critics, who accuse Harrison (like Heaney in *The Cure at Troy*) of attempting to create a new mythology: 'There is an arrogant tendency to conflate all of the big themes of the past hundred years into an enormous super myth: Orgreave to Auschwitz via Dresden, all aboard! One specific problem about this is that it is frankly offensive to imply that sacking someone is the same as butchering them alongside their families' (Keith Miller, *Times Literary Supplement*, 14 May 1999). The word *imply* is significant. Nowhere does Harrison's text say that this is so. However, the rhythm and narrative of the images make the connection, first between the redundant miners and Prometheus (they are delivered by cattle truck to a furnace in Europe, melted down and used to construct the gold statue) and then between the figure of Prometheus and the eagle, which in the myth ate his liver and which in the twentieth century represented the Third Reich and the perpe-trators of the Holocaust. This is where the layering of realist and filmic modes is most severely tested and where their 'plaiting' is secured by the metatheatrical device, the film within a film which includes both Hermes' commentary and the reactions of the Old Miner in his dilapi-dated seat in the old cinema. The effect of this eclectic narrative of suffering is two-fold. First, it certainly subverts translational norms and thus testifies to the capacity of the interplay of poetry and film to provoke shifts of imagination and regrouping of clusters of human sensibilities. The effect on the audience which experiences the verse-film is far more cumulative and coherent than can be communicated by a written account. Secondly, the film's representation of suffering on a European canvas puts recent history into a linked narrative and constitutes an intervention on the theme of European human identity and consciousness.

There remain, as with other types of interventionist translation, questions about the audience, especially their degree of critical aware-ness of the direction and force of the transposition from ancient to modern, and the extent to which submerged voices can be said to be given a hearing when the vehicle is the kind of film which is unlikely to be distributed for mass audiences and when the working-class communities which Harrison enacts, and from which he takes his vitality, are perhaps unlikely to know about the Prometheus myth and Aeschylus' refiguration of it. How many people in Barnsley, for instance, know about how Aeschylus handled the myth of Prometheus, or even about the myth itself? (Equally, it might be asked how many spectators at the Parish hall in Andersonstown, where Heaney's *The Cure at Troy* was staged, knew about Sophocles and Philoctetes, or even about Troy as an emblem in the Irish classical and nationalist traditions.) There are two ways in which such objections can be met. The play can be staged by and for the performers, as a Lehrstück, a learning transformation for the actors (as in some South African liberationist theatre, or in the TV film *Dockers*, 1999, which told the story of the Liverpool Dock strike and was scripted by some of the participants). Alternatively, spectator orientation can be integrated into the work itself. This is the technique chosen by Harrison and expressed through the figure of the boy who learns about the myth at school and tells his father who, distressed at his redundancy from the pit, throws the book on the fire. The subsequent layer of awareness, that of Aeschylus' play and its democratic context and culturally liberating effect, is conveyed through the spin-doctor Hermes and his communication direct to the film audience of Zeus' perspective on the danger represented by the poetry and ideas of the play. Both these aspects have been stressed by Harrison in discussion (Warburg Institute, London, 31 October 1999).

A criticism sometimes directed at modern discussions and theories about the reception of ancient texts is that debate often concentrates on how literature is received by society while ignoring ways in which society is received by literature. Harrison's film certainly rebuts any such claims. It is precisely because his treatments of the ancient myth and Aeschylus' play are filtered through his perceptions of both ancient and modern societies and of their cultural politics that his verse-film had such an electrifying impact on audiences. Not only is the audience introduced to the force of the myth and its role as a critique of contemporary society and politics, but those viewing the film are also challenged to identify and reassess their assumptions about the inter-relationship of national, European and global issues. This is an uncomfortable experience and some critics have reacted accordingly.

This process of re-examination of how society is received by art also raises acute questions about the nature of the equivalence implied in Harrison's translational techniques. In one sense, the use of modern technology and the genre of film might serve to detach the work from the Greek poetry and drama of the myth. However, it is also the case that Harrison, both as author and as director, structures the work round formal treatment of the relationship between Greek and modern. For example in Aeschylus the Chorus, which consists of the daughters of Oceanus, is sympathetic to the chained Prometheus, sometimes criticising but also consoling him, and remains loyally with him at the climactic earthquake at the end of the play. In Harrison the Chorus is developed from the group of women fish factory workers, then transformed into a group of agonised transfixed models with faces like Greek chorus masks whose role is to float on a raft which appears at various stages of the Europe-wide journey of the miners and of the Prometheus statue. The women of the Chorus have no verbal role. Their lament and the music which accompanies them warn of disaster, and visually they represent the Greek origins of the pessimistic vision communicated by the music.

Furthermore, Harrison uses metatheatre, the film within the film, to raise and partially to answer questions about how the 'real life' spectators are addressed and involved. The Staatsoper Munich production of Carl Orff's opera *Prometheus* (1968) used video techniques to project enlarged images of Prometheus' face onto the rock on which he was nailed, and Harrison drew on this experience to show that, in the case of the Old Miner, men projected onto a large screen could temporarily become like the heroes of Greek myth and drama. Filmic images could enable the viewer to gaze into the fires of Dresden and Hamburg and the ovens of Auschwitz and relate them to the horrors of Hiroshima, Nagasaki and the Balkans. In the Preface to *The Trackers of Oxyrhynchus*, Harrison discussed the space, light and theatrical mask which Greek theatre used to create a 'communal act of attention' (p. x). In the verse-film, it is the filmic images which create the space and movement, the interaction of fire and poetry which creates the light ('the light common to all', Aeschylus *Prometheus Bound* 1091-2).

The mask is the most problematic concept to translate across

137

genres. Harrison has used the theatrical mask in his staged versions
of Greek drama – '[the mask] represents a commitment to seeing
everything through the eyes that never close. It represents a commitment to going on speaking when the always open eyes have witnessed
something unspeakable. The masks must witness the unendurable ...
the mouth must continue to speak in situations where the human
being would be speechless or screaming and unable to articulate its
agony. The shared space and light allow this seeing and this speaking.
The shared light begs a common language.' All these aspects are
present in the *Prometheus* film, and in this sense the film itself fulfils
the function of the mask. This formal 'translation' across genres is also
a means towards fulfilling Harrison's broader aim (also set out in the
Preface to *Trackers*, p. xi) of finding out how the Greek spirit – and by
extension modern consciousness – coped with catastrophe.[11] The engagement of the *Prometheus* film with suffering and catastrophe is
unremitting. At the end there is a brief moment when it seems as
though the Hermes portrayed on the screen of the derelict cinema has
been defeated, blown up by the incendiary old miner. But of course,
Hermes is an immortal and survives, smirking.

So there has been no modern equivalent of a *deus ex machina*, that
reversal of fortune brought about by divine intervention (as in Sophocles' *Philoctetes* when Heracles resolves the impasse of trickery and
obligation and ensures the return of Philoctetes with the Greeks).
Nothing of this kind occurs in Harrison's *Prometheus*. It does not occur
either, of course, in Aeschylus' play, although Athenian spectators
would have known that in the myth Prometheus was eventually
released by Heracles – *Prometheus Unbound* being the concern of the
final play in the trilogy. In 'Fire and Poetry', his preface to *Prometheus*,
Harrison writes of the historical significance of Prometheus as a figure
of hope, a hope which is constantly tortured by tyranny, repression and
the infliction of suffering.

Harrison's work does not hold out false hope. Nevertheless, in
Labourers of Herakles (performed 1995; published 1996), the Spirit of
Phrynichos (played by Harrison himself) spoke of 'redeeming destruction through the power of art' (p. 143). Phrynichos was also the name
of an Athenian tragic poet who wrote at the turn of the sixth and fifth
centuries BCE. Some at least of his tragedies were about recent historical rather than mythical subjects, and one of his plays on the

contemporary *Capture of Miletos* caused so much distress to the Athenians that they fined him 'for reminding them of their own troubles'. Harrison's verse-film certainly performs this role. There is no claim that art has redeemed or will redeem. Indeed in a modern context (and bearing in mind Adorno's verdict that after Auschwitz there could be no poetry) it is almost as though the relationship between destruction and art has been inverted in this film and that the power of art may be redeemed through its engagement with the theme of destruction. In the film the contributing elements – film images, words, music, silences – all have a translational role. In this way, the genre of the verse-film creates a special kind of equivalence between ancient and modern realisations of Prometheus.

Coda

The true translator is he or she who ... plunges us into the
strangeness of the archaic world, into its distance and darkness
and who almost blinds us with the contemporaneity, with the
actuality of 'a light that screams across three thousand years'
(Logue's talismanic image).

Observer Review, 24 October 1999

Thus George Steiner summed up the paradox underlying the work of
the translators, version makers, adapters and poets discussed in this
book. The debates intensify about the shifting relationships which
particular poems and stagings have with the ancient texts and with
the expectations of readers and audiences. The capacity of ancient
poetry and drama to sharpen insights, frame identity and, if not to
change the world itself, at least to change perceptions of it, is still
electric. At the time of writing news is just out that the long awaited
John Barton *Tantalus*, a ten-play fifteen-hour cycle which tells the
story of the Trojan Wars, is at last to be staged, directed by Peter Hall,
initially at the Denver Centre for the Performing Arts in Colorado,
USA and then in 2001 on a European tour. Tony Harrison is engaged
on a project on Orpheus, and in March 2000 Glasgow theatre babel
gave a world premiere under the direction of Graham McLaren to
versions by Scottish playwrights of the tragedies *Oedipus* (David
Greig), *Electra* (Tom McGrath) and *Medea* (Liz Lochhead).[1]

The year 1999 was rich in new work energised by ancient poetry and
drama. One aspect was particularly important and suggests scope for
further debates. This was the publication and staging of work from the
last years of the life of Ted Hughes (1930-98). His final volumes of
poetry, *Tales from Ovid* and *Birthday Letters* (1998), renewed interest
in questions concerning the underlying relationship between a poet's
translations and the rest of his or her work. *Tales from Ovid*, based on

141

selections from Ovid's *Metamorphoses*, was adapted for the stage by Tim Supple and Simon Reade and performed by the Royal Shakespeare Company in 1999; another example of genre cross-over. Interest was intensified by the publication in 1999 of Hughes' version of Euripides' *Alcestis* – 'All you thought you had lost – she is here' – in which the style of the lines of Alcestis and the Chorus directs attention to the poetry of Sylvia Plath as well as of Euripides, and also by his version of Aeschylus' *Oresteia*, which was staged in two parts at the Royal National Theatre, directed by Katie Mitchell.

The stage adaptation of *Tales from Ovid* presented in acute form some of the issues already discussed in the chapters on genre cross-overs. Selections from Hughes' text were refigured so that indirect speech in the poems was put into direct speech and some of the narrative from the poems was assigned to specific voices – a female singer, a 'chorus' of cast members, a character directly expressing his or her actions or thought. Some of the most striking 'narratives' were actually non-verbal. Storytelling was achieved by sound effects (percussion being used both as a theatrical device and as narrative punctuation) and by movement and mime, and the ensemble developed its own language of physical theatre. These translational devices were interwoven with direct insertions from Ovid (sung in Latin). The stage version had to enact Hughes' narrative of Ovid's stories via the voice of the poet. The poet's own introduction to the 1997 translation stressed 'the swiftness and filmic economy of [Ovid's] narrative', 'the playful philosophical breadth of his detachment' and 'his strange yoking of incompatible moods'. The broadcast and audio-cassette readings by Hughes had seemed particularly appropriate to his personal voice, 'the current of human passion' and its metamorphosis in Ovid. The physicality and narrative strength of the staging actually enacted how Ovid via Hughes 'locates and captures the peculiar frisson of that event, when the all-too-human victim stumbles out into the mythic arena and is transformed'. This image of metamorphosis itself encapsulates the unlikely but in the event scintillating impact of this particular example of genre cross-over.

The staging of Hughes' *Oresteia* involved a different kind of double translation. It was a version of the Hughes translated onto the stage by the director Mitchell, the designer Vicki Mortimer and a strong cast as well as a version of the Aeschylus mediated via Hughes. Hughes' response to Aeschylus was to pare the Greek metre and syntax to the bone and sometimes, like Robert Browning, to roughen even Aeschylus' tone. He made the Watchman say (p. 5):

> Those who know too much, as I do, about this house,
> Let their tongue lie still – squashed flat.
> Under the foundations.

Hughes' diction is direct but almost without specific colloquial or contemporary allusion. The staging of the first part of the play, *The Home Guard* (that is, the *Agamemnon* of Aeschylus) added another layer of translation. The Chorus, in wheelchairs, wore poppies and after Agamemnon's death red berets, like members of the Parachute regiment. They were attended by uniformed nurses. The movement and focus of the staging were governed by the shape of the Cottesloe Theatre's playing space, which had the audience ranged on both long sides. At one end was a large sliding door to the palace. This also served as a 'commentary' screen for black-and-white film of end-of-war celebrations and later for video close-ups of Iphigenia and Clytemnestra. The 'carpet' on which Agamemnon trod in order to enter the palace consisted of a collage of the mostly red dresses of small children (possibly alluding to the image of the red dress of a child in the film *Schindler's List*).

Costume was modern but eclectic, with Agamemnon dressed as a guerrilla fighter and Clytemnestra in a formal dress, emblazoned with a poppy design. Aegisthus, in dinner jacket, danced with her in a pastiche of the country-house ambience of T.S. Eliot's *The Family Reunion* (a re-enactment of the *Oresteia* theme, revived by the Royal Shakespeare Company in 1999). Music was also eclectic, with Balkan resonances countered by Chopin. The production also followed the recent trend of enacting the words of the Chorus. Here, as the sacrifice of Iphigenia was lamented, she appeared, gagged, and as she remained viewing from a gallery her image was projected onto the screen/palace door. This alluded to the emphasis in Aeschylus, played with by Hughes, on the images associated with the tongue. Furthermore, at points in the play, low-key verbal delivery functioned as a kind of 'mask' for emotion and diverted attention towards the theatrical impact of the design, movement and multi-media aspects of the production. The programme included extracts from Ted Hughes' text, photographs of children's abandoned shoes and toys, with bullet holes ringed and the 'exhibits' numbered as for a criminal investigation. This acted as the equivalent of an intervention in the audience's reception of the play, a variant perhaps on the techniques used in foyer exhibitions for Müller's *Medeamaterial*.

As a theatrical experience the staging was, although striking, strangely unsatisfying, not because it was as one critic described it 'a glib anti-war morality play' but rather because at times the cutting edge seemed 'masked', not as in the Greek convention to intensify the effect, but instead to dissipate it in a pastiche of twentieth-century referents. The staging seemed both to dragoon the spectators into responding to a particular agenda of equivalences between ancient and modern and yet to render those equivalences incoherent, both politically and aesthetically. When compared with the staging of *Tales from Ovid*, it demonstrated perhaps that success in transplanting to the stage a translation originally created for the page depends much less on genre equivalence than on allowing the poetry to be refigured in interaction with the staging, rather than against it. In the end, the staging of Hughes' *Oresteia* used modern signs which had a meaning in themselves but which did not enhance or mesh with Hughes' text. So in this sequence translation was less a double mediation than a triangular activity, with Hughes' version of Aeschylus set against Mitchell and Mortimer's version of Hughes. There is a sense in which Hughes' perception for the Chorus that 'Pity is like a butterfly in a fist as the knuckles whiten' needs no visual effects, simply because it is itself a visual image.

A critical study of the role of classical referents in Hughes' late work must be a priority. More broadly, the staging and critical reception of his *Oresteia* suggest that a watershed in the translation of Greek drama has been passed. The recuperation of ancient poetry into modern theatre has progressed beyond the point where simple contemporary allusions, verbal or non-verbal, are a significant aspect of 'equivalence' or, indeed, are any longer necessary in order for the audience to be convinced. Rather, equivalence grows from a web of translational practices, both verbal and visual, which gradually shift norms. To transpose Hughes' own metaphor, ancient poetry mutates into an experience which is both devastatingly familiar and magically transformative.

144

Notes

1. The Battles of Translation

1. Edwin Morgan, *Crossing the Border: Essays on Scottish Literature* (Carcanet 1990) 71.

2. Recent publications include Josephine Balmer, *Classical Women Poets* (Bloodaxe Books 1996) and *Sappho: Poems and Fragments* (Bloodaxe Books 1992).

3. M. Arnold 'On Translating Homer' (1860-1) in R.H. Super (ed.), *On the Classical Tradition: The Complete Prose Works of Matthew Arnold,* vol. 1 (Ann Arbor 1960) 102.

4. M. Silk, *The Iliad* (Cambridge 1987) 54-69.

5. M. Reck, Introduction to *The Iliad* (HarperCollins 1994) 15.

6. K. Myrsiades (ed.), *Approaches to Teaching Homer's Iliad and Odyssey* (Modern Language Association of America 1987) 3-5.

7. H. Lloyd-Jones, 'Welcome Homer!', *New York Review of Books* (14 February 1991).

8. H. Lloyd-Jones, 'On Translations of Epic and Drama', *Classical Survivals* (Duckworth 1982) 137-8.

9. Lloyd-Jones (1991).

10. Discussed by E.R. Dodds, introduction to Jean Smith and Arnold Toynbee (eds), *Gilbert Murray: An Unfinished Autobiography* (George Allen & Unwin 1960) 3-19.

11. D. West, 'Translating the *Aeneid*', *Omnibus* 14 (1987).

12. D. West, *Virgil: The Aeneid* (Penguin Books 1990) xii.

13. D.S. Carne-Ross, 'Translation and Transposition' in W. Arrowsmith and R. Shattuck (eds), *The Craft and Context of Translation* (Austin, Texas 1961) 20.

14. Seamus Heaney, *Beowulf: A New Translation* (Faber & Faber 1999) ix.

15. Eric Anderson, *The Guardian* (26 January 2000).

16. Balmer (1996) 22.

2. Reverence and Subversion in
Nineteenth-Century Translation

1. W. Toynbee (ed.), *The Diaries of William Charles Macready 1833-1851*, vol. 2 (Chapman & Hall 1912) 289, quoted Hall (1999).

2. W.E. Gladstone, *Studies in Homer and the Homeric Age*, vol. 3 (Oxford University Press 1858) 616.

3. R. Tyrell, 'Translation as Fine Art', *Hermathena* 6 no. 13 (Dublin 1887) 147-58.

4. George Stillman Hillard, *North American Review* (July 1842).

5. C.A. Bristed, *The Knickerbocker* (1845).

6. Elvan Kintner (ed.), *The Letters of Robert Browning and Elizabeth Barrett: 1845-1846* (Belknap Press of Harvard University Press 1969) 233, discussed in Yopie Prins, 'Elizabeth Barrett and Robert Browning and the *Difference* of Translation', *Victorian Poetry* vol. 29, no. 4 (Winter 1991) 435-51.

7. Mary L. Bruce, *Anna Swanwick: A Memoir and Recollections 1813-1899* (T. Fisher Unwin 1903) 19.

8. Quoted by Bruce, op. cit., p. 34.

3. The View from Translation: Image,
Window and Dissection

1. For an outline chronology of HD's life and major works see R. Blau DuPlessis, *The Career of That Struggle* (Harvester Press 1986) xix-xxi.

2. For a detailed catalogue of HD's use of classical referents see E. Gregory, *HD and Hellenism* (CUP 1997) 233-58.

3. Unpublished text in Beinecke Library, Yale University, quoted in Patricia Moyer, 'Getting Personal about Euripides' in J.P. Hallett and T. van Nortwick (eds), *Compromising Traditions: The Personal Voice in Classical Scholarship* (Routledge 1997) 109-10.

4. Christopher Logue, 'The Art of Poetry LXVI (Interview)', *Paris Review* 127, Summer 1993, 254, quoted and discussed in Underwood (1998) 56-7.

4. Translation as Critique and Intervention

1. 'Horaz Satiren II I' in *Die Umsiedlerin oder das Leben auf dem Lande*, Texte 3 (Rotbuch 1975).

2. See Seidensticker (1992) 327-67.

3. See Lenin's Fourth Thesis on proletarian culture: V.I. Lenin, *Collected Works* (Moscow 1966) XXXI 317, quoted in Seidensticker (1992) 350.

4. Quoted and translated by Seidensticker (1992) 352.

5. The performance history and contexts of Brecht's *Antigone* are discussed in Flashar (1991) 186-91.

6. Quoted in Seidensticker (1992) 351.

7. For discussion see M. Blumberg and D. Walder eds, *South African Theatre and/as Intervention* (Rodopi 1989) especially 1-24.

8. Heiner Müller, *Germania* ed. Sylvère Lotringer, trans. Bernard and Caroline Schütze (Alexander Verlag 1992) 67, 71.

9. Heiner Müller, *Jenseits der Nation* (Rotbuch 1991) trans. and quoted Kalb (1998) 15.

10. Oscar Mandel (trans.; in collaboration with Maria Kelsen Feder), *Philoctetes and the Fall of Troy: Plays, Documents, Iconography, Interpretations* (University of Nebraska Press 1981) 222-50.

11. For further discussion, see David Barnett, *Literature versus Theatre: Textual Problems and Theatrical Realization in the Later Plays of Heiner Müller* (Peter Lang 1998) especially 34-40.

12. A.C. Verloren van Themaat, translated by P.J. Conradie. Source: private correspondence.

13. For discussion, with bibliography, of the politically motivated reworking of Greek tragedy in South Africa at this time, see Mezzabotta (2000).

14. N. Mandela, *Long Walk to Freedom* (Abacus 1995) 541.

15. For a detailed account of the production in the context of South African culture and politics, see Mezzabotta (2000).

16. See Banning (1997) 55-87, discussed in Mezzabotta (2000) and in L. Hardwick, *The Theatrical Review as a Primary Source for the Modern Reception of Greek Drama: A Preliminary Evaluation* (http://www2.open.ac.uk/ClassicalStudies/GreekPlays/Reviews.html).

5. Translation and Cultural Politics: The Irish Dimension

1. *Times Literary Supplement*, 8 October 1999.

2. *The New Oxford Book of Irish Verse* ed. Thomas Kinsella (OUP 1986), no. 217, pp. 320-1.

3. ibid. no. 152, p. 218.

4. ibid., no. 152.

6. Walcott's Philoctete: Imaging the Post-Colonial Condition

1. See E. Wilson, *The Wound and the Bow* (1st ed. 1941, rev. ed. 1952, reprinted in University Paperbacks series 1961) 247ff.

2. See Oliver Taplin, 'Derek Walcott's *Omeros* and Derek Walcott's Homer', *Arion* 3rd series 2, (1991) 214-16 for discussion and criticism of the principles of organisation.

3. For discussion and examples, see M.W. Edwards, *The Iliad: A Commentary,* vol. V: *Books 17-20* (Cambridge University Press 1991) 24-41.

4. For detailed discussion see R. Terada, *Derek Walcott's Poetry: American Mimicry* (Northeastern University Press 1993).

5. D. Walcott, *Another Life* (Farrar, Straus & Giroux 1973).

6. 'The muse of History' (1974) collected in D. Walcott, *What the Twilight Says: Essays* (Faber & Faber 1998) 36-64.

7. Discussed J. Ramazani 'The Wound of History: Walcott's *Omeros* and the Post-Colonial Poetics of Affliction', *Proceedings of the Modern Literature Association* 112(3) (May 1997) 405-15.

8. Derek Walcott, *The Antilles: Fragments of Epic Memory* The Nobel Lecture (Farrar, Straus & Giroux 1993) 30.

9. For discussion see Robert D. Hamner, *Derek Walcott* (Twayne Publishers 1981) and Tevada (1993).

10. *Journal of Inter-American Studies and World Affairs* 16.6-7 (1974) 3-13.

11. Ibid.

12. See for example Frantz Fanon, *The Wretched of the Earth*, trans. Constance Farrington (Grove, 1963) 222-3 and Bill Ashcroft, Gareth Griffiths and Helen Tiffin, *The Empire Writes Back: Theory and Practice in Post-Colonial Literatures* (Routledge 1989) especially pp. 4-5 and 33-37.

13. See Lorna Hardwick, 'Classical Distances', *One World Many Voices: Proceedings of the ICDE Conference*, Birmingham, vol. 1 (1995) 283-6; 'A Daidalos in the Late-Modern Age? Transplanting Homer into Derek Walcott's The Odyssey: A Stage Version', in L. Hardwick and S. Ireland, *Selected Proceedings of the January Conference: The Reception of Classical Texts and Images* (Open University, Milton Keynes 1996) 232-52 (published also on the World Wide Web: http://www.open.ac.uk/Arts/CC96/hardwick.htm); S.P. Morris, *Daidalos and the Origins of Greek Art* (Princeton University Press 1992); M.L. West, *East of Helicon* (Oxford 1997); W. Burkert, *The Orientalising Revolution: Near Eastern Influence in Greek Culture in the Early Archaic Age* (Harvard University Press 1992).

7. Translating Genres (i)

1. Demodocus in Derek Walcott's *The Odyssey: A Stage Version* II.IV (Faber & Faber 1993) 122.

2. For discussion of the evidence concerning ancient epic in performance and recitation, see O. Taplin, *Homeric Soundings* (Oxford University Press 1992); R. Thomas, 'The Place of the Poet in Archaic Society' in A. Powell (ed.), *The Greek World* (Routledge 1995) 106-17; G. Nagy, *Poetry as Performance: Homer and Beyond* (Cambridge University Press, 1996).

3. For discussion see B. Goward, *Telling Tragedy: Narrative Techniques in Aeschylus, Sophocles and Euripides* (Duckworth 1999) especially 1-54.

4. Source: Martin Wylde (Director), interview November 1999, for the

Research Project on *The Reception of the Texts and Images of Ancient Greece in Late Twentieth-Century Drama and Poetry in English* (http://www2.open.ac.uk/ClassicalStudies/GreekPlays).

5. P. Rabinowitz, 'Truth in Fiction: A Re-Examination of Audiences', *Critical Enquiry* 4 (1977) 121-42.

6. Source: interview with Lorna Hardwick, excerpted in Video II 'Truth, Imagination and Value' in *Homer: Poetry and Society* (BBC/Open University Productions 1992).

7. For detailed discussion of the formal, discursive and contextual relationship between Homer's *Odyssey* and Walcott's *Stage Version* see Hardwick (1996) 232-52.

8. See H. Bhabha, *The Location of Culture* (Routledge 1994) 212.

9. For further discussion see Marilyn Katz, *Penelope's Renown: Meaning and Indeterminacy in the Odyssey* (Princeton 1991).

10. H. Roisman, 'Penelope's Indignation', *Transactions of the American Philological Association* 117 (1987) 59-68.

11. Source: interview with Lorna Hardwick, 1992, cited in n. 6 above. On Walcott's alleged insensitivity to gender issues see Elaine Savory Fido, 'Walcott and Sexual Politics: Macho Conventions Shape the Moon', *Literary Half Yearly* XXVI (Jan. 1985) 43-60 and in *Journal of Commonwealth Literature*, vol. xxi, no. 1 (Oxford 1986).

12. Source: *Making Hay*, Channel 4 TV (May 1993).

13. A. Sinfield (1992) especially ch. 2, 'Cultural Materialism'.

14. Richard Buxton, *Imaginary Greece: The Contexts of Mythology* (CUP, 1994) 219.

8. Translating Genres (ii)

1. For an overview, see Jane Davidson Reid, *The Oxford Guide to Classical Mythology and the Arts 1300-1990s* (Oxford University Press 1993).

2. See Todd Bender, *Gerard Manley Hopkins: The Classical Background and Critical Reception of His Work* (Johns Hopkins University Press 1966) 56-7.

3. F. Macintosh in Easterling (1997) 305-6.

4. For discussion in the context of twentieth-century Greece, see Platon Mavromoustakos, 'Ancient Greek Drama on the Modern Stage: The Question of Theatrical Space' in *A Stage for Dionysus: Theatrical Space and Ancient Drama* (Athens 1999) 177-89.

5. For discussion of recent stagings of versions of *Prometheus Bound* see L. Hardwick 'Placing Prometheus' in L. Hardwick (ed.), *Tony Harrison's Poetry, Drama and Film: The Classical Dimension* (Milton Keynes 2000 forthcoming, also published electronically: http://www.open.ac.uk/Arts/classtud).

6. Harrison, 'Fire and Poetry', preface to *Prometheus* (1998) vii-viii.

7. Jonathan Miller, quoted in Jonathan Price, 'Jonathan Miller directs Robert Lowell's *Prometheus*', *Yale Theatre* I (Spring 1968) 40.

8. Harrison (1998) xxvii.

9. Jack J. Jorgens, *Shakespeare on Film* (Indiana University Press 1977) also discussed in Kenneth MacKinnon, *Greek Tragedy into Film* (Croom Helm, 1986) 19-20.

10. Ibid., p. 126 and further discussed in relation to a range of films of Greek tragedies in K. MacKinnon, 'Film Adaptation and the Myth of Textual Fidelity' in L. Hardwick (ed.), *Tony Harrison's Poetry, Drama and Film: The Classical Dimension* (Milton Keynes 2000 forthcoming, also published electronically: *http://www.open.ac.uk /Arts/classtud*).

11. See also Peter Robinson 'Facing up to the Unbearable: The Mythical Method in Tony Harrison's Film-Poems' in L. Hardwick (ed.), *Tony Harrison's Poetry, Drama and Film: The Classical Dimension* (Milton Keynes 2000 forthcoming, also published electronically:
http://www.open.ac.uk /Arts/classtud).

Coda

1. These and other new translations, versions and poems will be documented and reviewed by the Reception of Classical Texts Research Project at the Open University as part of its database published electronically at http://www2.open.ac.uk/ClassicalStudies/GreekPlays.

Select Bibliography

Texts and translations

Balmer, J. (trans. & intr.), *Classical Women Poets* (Bloodaxe Books 1996).

Day Lewis, C., *The Aeneid of Virgil* (Oxford University Press 1966).

Doolittle, H.D. in L.L. Martz (ed.), *HD: Collected Poems 1912-1944* (Carcanet Press 1984); C. Laity (ed.), *Paint It Today* (New York University Press 1992).

Douglas, G., *Virgil's 'Aeneid' translated into Scottish Verse*, ed. D.F.C. Coldwell, 4 vols (Blackwood & Sons 1957-64).

Duffy, C.A., *The World's Wife* (Macmillan 1999).

Fagles, R. (trans.), *Sophocles: The Three Theban Plays* (Penguin 1984); *Homer: Iliad* (Viking Penguin 1990); *Homer: Odyssey* (Viking Penguin 1996).

Fitzgerald, R. (trans.), *The Odyssey* (Anchor Press/Doubleday 1961); *The Iliad* (Anchor Press 1974).

Friel, B., *Selected Plays* (Faber 1984).

Gransden, K.W. (ed.), *Virgil in English* (Penguin 1996).

Harrison, T., *The Oresteia* in *Theatre Works 1973-1985* (Penguin 1985); *The Trackers of Oxyrhynchus* (Faber & Faber 1990); *The Gaze of the Gorgon* (Bloodaxe Books 1992); *The Labourers of Herakles* Plays 3 (Faber & Faber 1996); *Prometheus* (Faber & Faber 1998).

Heaney, S., *The Cure at Troy: A Version of Sophocles' 'Philoctetes'* (Faber & Faber 1990); *The Spirit Level* (Faber & Faber 1996); (trans.) *Beowulf* (Faber & Faber 1999).

Hofmann, M. and Lasdun, J. (eds), *After Ovid: New Metamorphoses* (Faber & Faber 1994).

Hughes, T., *Tales from Ovid* (Faber & Faber 1997); *Euripides: Alcestis* (Faber & Faber 1999); *Aeschylus: The Oresteia* (Faber & Faber 1999).

Kennelly, B., *Antigone* (Bloodaxe 1996); *Medea* (Bloodaxe 1991); *The Trojan Women* (Bloodaxe 1993).

Keynes, G. (ed.), *The Poetical Works of Rupert Brooke*, 2nd ed. (Faber & Faber 1970).

Lattimore, R. (trans.), *The Iliad* (University of Chicago Press 1961); *The Odyssey* (Harper Perennial 1965, 1991).

Logue, C., *War Music: An Account of Books 16 to 19 of Homer's Iliad* (Faber & Faber 1988); *Kings: An Account of Books 1 and 2 of Homer's Iliad*, rev. ed.

151

Select Bibliography

(Faber & Faber 1992); *The Husbands: An Account of books 3 and 4 of Homer's Iliad* (Faber & Faber 1994); *Selected Poems*, chosen and arranged by Christopher Reid (Faber & Faber 1996).

Longley, M., *The Ghost Orchid* (Jonathan Cape 1995); *Broken Dishes* (Abbey Press 1998).

Mahon, D., *The Bacchae: After Euripides* (Gallery Books 1991).

Mandel, O. (trans. in collaboration with M.K. Feder), *Philoctetes and the Fall of Troy: Plays, Documents, Iconography, Interpretations* (University of Nebraska Press 1981).

McGuinness, F., *Electra* (Gallery Books 1991).

Morgan, E., *Phaedra* (tr. From the French into Scots, Carcanet 2000).

Muldoon, P. with Martin, R. (trans.), *The Birds* (Gallery Books 1999).

Müller, H., 'Geschichten von Homer' in *Die Umsiedlerin, oder das Leben auf dem Lande* (Berlin, 1975), English translation in C. Weber (ed. and trans.), *The Battle: Plays, Prose, Poems* (New York 1989); *Verkommenes Ufer Medeamaterial Landschaft mit Argonauten*, published text in *Herzstück, Texte 7* (Rotbuch 1983).

Oswald, P., *Odysseus* (Oberon Books 1999).

Owen, W., in J. Stallworthy (ed.), *The Poems of Wilfred Owen* (Hogarth Press 1985).

Paulin, T., *The Riot Act: A Version of Sophocles' Antigone* (Faber & Faber 1985); *Seize the Fire* (Faber & Faber 1990).

Poole, A. and Maule, J. (eds), *The Oxford Book of Classical Verse in Translation* (Oxford University Press 1995).

Reck, M., *The Iliad* (Harper Collins 1994).

Rieu, E.V., *The Odyssey* (Penguin 1946, rev. D.C.H. Rieu and P.V. Jones 1991); *The Iliad* (Penguin 1950, 1966).

Rosenberg, I., *The Collected Works of Isaac Rosenberg: Poetry, Prose, Letters, Paintings and Drawings*, ed. I. Parsons (Chatto & Windus 1979).

Shewring, W., *The Odyssey* (Oxford University Press 1980).

Steiner, G. (ed.), *Homer in English* (Penguin 1996).

Teevan, C., *Iph* (Gallery Books 1991).

Vellacott, P. (trans.), *Aeschylus: Prometheus Bound; The Suppliants; Seven Against Thebes* (Penguin 1964); *Euripides: The Bacchae and Other Plays* (Penguin 1972).

Walcott, D., *Collected Poems 1948-1984* (Noonday Press 1986); *Omeros* (Faber & Faber 1990); *The Odyssey: A Stage Version* (Faber & Faber 1993).

Wertenbaker, T. (trans.), *The Thebans* (Faber & Faber 1992).

West, D., *Virgil: The Aeneid* (Penguin 1990).

Yeats, W.B., *The Collected Poems of W.B.Yeats* (Macmillan 1968).

Select Bibliography

Critical works

Arrowsmith, W. and Shattuck, R. (eds), *The Craft and Context of Translation* (University of Texas Press 1961 and New York Anchor Books 1964, including additional material).

Banning, Y., '(Re)Viewing *Medea*: Cultural Perceptions and Gendered Consciousness in Reviewers' Responses to New South African Theatre', *South African Theatre Journal* II, 1&2 (1997) 55-87.

Barnett, D., *Literature versus Theatre: Textual Problems and Theatrical Realization in the Later Plays of Heiner Müller* (Peter Lang 1998).

Bassnett, S., 'The Meek or the Mighty: Re-Appraising the Role of the Translator' in R. Alvarez and M. Vidal (eds), *Translation, Power, Subversion* (Multilingual Matters Ltd 1996) 10-24.

Bassnett-McGuire, S., *Translation Studies* (Methuen 1980).

Byrne, S. (ed.), *Tony Harrison: Loiner* (Clarendon Press 1997); *H, v., & O: The Poetry of Tony Harrison* (Manchester University Press 1998).

Canitz, A.E. Christa, 'In our awyn language: The Nationalist Agenda of Gavin Douglas' *Eneados*', *Vergilius* 1996, 42, 25-37.

Cronin, M., *Translating Ireland: Translation, Languages, Cultures* (Cork University Press 1996).

Deane, S. (ed. and intro.), *The Field Day Anthology of Irish Writing* (Field Day 1991).

Eagleton, T., *News from Nowhere* 9 (1991) 93-5, reprinted in S. Regan (ed.). *The Eagleton Reader* (Blackwell 1998) 374-77.

Easterling, P.E. (ed.), *The Cambridge Companion to Greek Tragedy* (Cambridge University Press 1997).

Egan, D. (trans.), *Medea* (Kavanagh Press 1991).

Flashar, H., *Inszenierung der Antike: das griechische Drama auf der Bühne der Neuzeit, 1585-1990* (C.H. Beck 1991).

Gilmour, R., *The Victorian Period: The Intellectual and Cultural Context of English Literature, 1830-1890* (Longman 1993).

Hall, E., *Inventing the Barbarian: Greek Self-Definition Through Tragedy* (Oxford University Press 1991); '1845 and All That: Singing Greek Tragedy on the London Stage' in M. Wyke and M. Biddiss (eds), *The Uses and Abuses of Antiquity* (Peter Lang 1999) 37-55.

Hardwick, L.P., 'Convergence and Divergence in Reading Homer' in C. Emlyn-Jones, L. Hardwick and J. Purkis (eds), *Homer: Readings and Images* (Duckworth 1992) 227-48; 'A Daidalos in the Late-Modern Age? Transplanting Homer into Derek Walcott's *"The Odyssey: A Stage Version"*, *Selected Proceedings – Conference on 'The Reception of Classical Texts and Images*', 3 and 4 January 1996, held at The Open University, Milton Keynes, UK (Milton Keynes 1996, and electronically available at http://www.open.ac.uk/Arts/CC96/ccfrontpage/hardwick.htm); 'Reception as Simile: The Poetics of Reversal in Homer and Derek Walcott', *International Journal of the Classical Tradition*, vol. 3 (Winter 1997) 326-38; 'Women, Translation and Empowerment' in J. Bellamy, A. Laurence and G. Perry (eds), *Women, Scholarship and Criticism* (Manchester University Press 2000a); 'Theatres of the Mind: Greek Tragedy in Women's Writing in England in the Nineteenth Century' in Lorna Hardwick, Pat Easterling, Stanley Ireland, Nick Lowe, Fiona Macintosh (eds), *Selected Proceedings – Conference on 'Theatre: Ancient and Modern'*, January 1999, held at The Open University, Milton Keynes, UK (Milton Keynes 2000b, electronically available at http://www.open.ac.uk/Arts/CC99/ccfrontpage.htm); 'Translations, Adaptations and Versions of Homer in the Nineteenth and Twentieth Centuries' in T. Hermans et al. (eds), *Ein Internationales Handbuch zur Übersetzungsforschung* (Walter de Gruyter, Berlin/New York forthcoming 2000/1).

Hermans, T. (ed.), *The Manipulation of Literature* (Croom Helm 1985); 'Translational Norms and Correct Translations' in Kitty M. van Leuven-Zwart and Ton Naaijkens (eds), *Translation Studies: The State of the Art* (Rodopi 1991); 'Norms and the Determination of Translation: A Theoretical Approach' in R. Alvarez and M. Vidal (eds), *Translation, Power, Subversion* (Multilingual Matters Ltd 1996) 25-51.

Jenkyns, R., *The Victorians and Ancient Greece* (Blackwell 1980).

Kalb, J., *The Theatre of Heiner Müller* (CUP 1998).

Kelly, L.G., *The True Interpreter: A History of Translation Theory and Practice in the West* (Blackwell 1979).

Lefevere, A. (ed.), *Translation / History / Culture: A Sourcebook* (Routledge 1992).

Liversidge, M. and Edwards, C., *Imagining Rome: British Artists and Rome in the Nineteenth Century* (Merrell Holberton 1996).

McDonald, M., 'Seamus Heaney's *Cure at Troy*: Politics and Poetry', *Classics Ireland* 3 (1996) 129-40; *Ancient Sun, Modern Light: Greek Drama on the Modern Stage* (Columbia University Press 1992).

Meir, C., 'Irish Poetic Drama: Seamus Heaney's *The Cure at Troy*' in J. Genet and E. Hellegouarc'h (eds), *Studies on the Contemporary Irish Theatre* (Actes du Colloque de Caen 1991) 67-8.

Mezzabotta, M.R., 'Ancient Greek Drama in the New South Africa' in Lorna Hardwick, Pat Easterling, Stanley Ireland, Nick Lowe, Fiona Macintosh (eds), *Selected Proceedings – Conference on 'Theatre: Ancient and Modern'* 1999, held at The Open University, Milton Keynes, UK (Milton Keynes 2000, electronically available at http://www.open.ac.uk/Arts/CC99/ccfrontpage.htm).

Murray, G., *An Unfinished Autobiography*, ed. J. Smith and A. Toynbee (George Allen & Unwin 1960).

O'Rawe, D., '(Mis)Translating Tragedy: Irish Poets and Greek Plays' in Lorna Hardwick, Pat Easterling, Stanley Ireland, Nick Lowe, Fiona Macintosh (eds), *Selected Proceedings – Conference on 'Theatre: Ancient and Modern'*, 5 and 6 January 1999, held at The Open University, Milton Keynes, UK (Milton Keynes 2000, electronically available at http://www.open.ac.uk/Arts/CC99/ccfrontpage.htm).

Patsalidis, S. and Sakellaridou, E. (eds), *(Dis)placing Classical Greek Theatre* (University Studio Press 1999).

Paulin, T., *Ireland and the English Crisis* (Bloodaxe Books 1984).

Ramazani, J., 'The Wound of History: Walcott's *Omeros* and the Post-Colonial Poetics of Affliction', *Publications of the Modern Literature Association* 112(3), May 1997, pp. 405-15.

Richards, S., 'In the Border Country: Greek Tragedy and Contemporary Irish Drama' in C.C. Barfoot and Rias van der Doel (eds), *Ritual Remembering: History, Myth and Politics and Anglo-Irish Drama* (Rodopi 1995) 191-200.

Roche, A., 'Ireland's *Antigones*: Tragedy North and South' in Michael Kenneally (ed.), *Cultural Contexts and Literary Idioms in Contemporary Irish Literature* (Colin Smyth 1998) 221-50.

Seidensticker, B., 'The Political use of Antiquity in the Literature of the German Democratic Republic', *Illinois Classical Studies*, vol. 17 (1992) 347-67.

Simon, S., *Gender in Translation: Cultural Identity and the Politics of Transmission* (Routledge 1996).

Sinfield, A., *Faultlines: Cultural Materialism and the Politics of Dissident Reading* (OUP 1992).

Stanford, W.B., *Ireland and the Classical Tradition* (Allen Figgis 1976).

Steiner, G., *The Death of Tragedy* (Faber & Faber 1961, reprinted OUP 1980); *Antigones* (Clarendon Press 1984); *After Babel: Aspects of Language and Translation* (OUP 1998).

Stray, C.A., *Classics Transformed: Schools, Universities and Society in England, 1830-1960* (Clarendon Press 1998).

Terada, R., *Derek Walcott's Poetry: American Mimicry* (Northeastern University Press 1993).

Toury, G., *Descriptive Translation Studies and Beyond* (John Benjamin's Publishing Co. 1995)

Tudeau-Clayton, M., 'Richard Carew, William Shakespeare, and the Politics of Translating Virgil in Early Modern England and Scotland', *International Journal of the Classical Tradition*, vol. 5, no. 4 (Spring 1999; published Spring 2000), 507-27.

Turner, F.M., *The Greek Heritage in Victorian Britain* (Yale University Press 1981); 'Antiquity in Victorian Contexts', *Browning Institute Studies* 10, 1-4 (1982); 'Why the Greeks and not the Romans in Victorian Britain' in G.W. Clarke (ed.), *Rediscovering Hellenism: The Hellenic Inheritance and the English Imagination* (Cambridge University Press 1989) 61-81; *Contesting Cultural Authority* (Cambridge University Press 1993).

Underwood, S., *English Translators of Homer* (Northcote House 1998); 'Harrison's Aeschylus and Logue's Homer', *Dialogos* no. 5 (1998) 76-100.

Venuti, L., *Rethinking Translation: Discourse, Subjectivity, Ideology* (1992); *The Translator's Invisibility* (Routledge 1995).

Welch, R. *Changing States: Transformations in Modern Irish Writing* (Routledge 1993).

Wilmer, S.E., 'Seamus Heaney and the tragedy of stasis' in S. Patsalidis and E. Sakellaridou (eds), *(Dis)placing Classical Greek Theatre* (University Studio Press 1999) 221-31.

Wyke, M., *Projecting the Past: Ancient Rome, Cinema and History* (Routledge 1997).

Wyke, M. and Biddiss, M. (eds), *The Uses and Abuses of Antiquity* (Peter Lang 1999).

Index